monsoonbooks

SINGAPORE GIRL

Ex-seminarian and ex-... kardt joined the Peace Corp... ...try of Sierra Leone, better known as "The White Man's Grave", after which he embarked on a trans-African motorcycle trip with two other hardy idiots. After a second stint in the Peace Corps, planting sugar cane in the Brazilian Amazon, he joined a friend in Manila for a two-thousand-mile sailboat trip to Jakarta. A stopover in Singapore led him into the bawdy spectacle of 1970s Bugis Street – a world long vanished today.

Eckardt settled in Thailand where he's lived for thirty years with his Thai wife and four children. He is the author of two novels, four collections of stories, and a bestselling book of profiles called *Bangkok People*.

Singapore Girl
A MEMOIR

JAMES ECKARDT

monsoon

monsoonbooks

Published in 2006
by Monsoon Books Pte Ltd
106 Jalan Hang Jebat #02–14, Singapore 139527
www.monsoonbooks.com.sg

ISBN-13: 978-981-05-6234-2
ISBN-10: 981-05-6234-9

Printed in Singapore

10 09 08 07 06   1 2 3 4 5 6 7 8 9

For Milly

"I once loved a girl,
  Her skin it was bronze.
  With the innocence of a lamb,
  She was gentle as a fawn.
  I courted her proudly
  But now she is gone,
  Gone like the season she's taken.

Ah, my friends from the prison,
  They ask unto me:
  How good, how good
  Does it feel to be free?
  And I answer them most mysteriously:
  Are birds free from the chains of the skyway?"

– Bob Dylan, "Ballad in Plain D"

Contents

Prologue

On a bright, crisp, cloudless autumn day – October 12, 1972, my twenty-sixth birthday – we were speeding along the FDR Drive, the East River sparkling beside us and the low skyline of Brooklyn beyond, when the LSD kicked in.

Erik was driving, Alison and Fran in the cab with him, Percy, Jon and I stretched out in the bed of the Ford pickup, goggle-eyed and giggling. We were tripping to the Catskills supposedly – hilariously – to ride horses. Little did we realize what the next sixteen hours would hold ...

But first a bit of background.

In 1969, the four of us – Erik Hansen, Percy Jones, Jon Newfield and I – had joined the Peace Corps, dispatched to the tiny West African country of Sierra Leone, affectionately known as "The White Man's Grave" and perennial contender for the title "Poorest Country on Earth".

Our Peace Corps group in Sierra Leone could be roughly divided into two groups: idealists and drunks. The idealists couldn't take life in poor remote villages – no electricity, no running water – and fled home. We drunks loved it. The dope was good too.

Out of our original group of twenty, nine lasted the two years, growing crazier by the month. The craziest of us all was Erik Hansen, our Bull Goose Loony.

Erik was a Zonian. Having grown up in the Panama Canal Zone, he was a bit more advanced than the rest of us. When we were puffing our first cigarette, he was smoking joints. When we were stealing our first kiss, he was prowling the brothels of Panama City. Erik was having so much fun his father banished him to a military boarding school in Florida. To celebrate his release, Erik rode his 500cc Norton Commando to New Orleans, tripping all the way on acid. For the rest of us, our first ride on a motorcycle was aboard the little 65cc motorbikes we were issued in Sierra Leone.

Broad-shouldered, barrel-chested, sandy-haired, the All-American boy, Erik even *looked* different from us. He was the most successful too. While Jon built a school in his village of Mahara and I was the Chicken King of the Northern Province, Erik enlisted the help of Taiwanese aid experts and introduced irrigated paddy rice to his village – making Mapaki the only place to buy rice during the "hungry season".

Erik was the daredevil of our group; he would launch himself into outrageously dangerous stunts and, worse, convince you to follow him. Near my village, for example, was the famous Bumbuna Waterfall – a three hundred-foot-tall roaring wall of white water. Erik decided to play with it. Perching himself on a rocky precipice right at the foot of the waterfall, he told me he wanted to dive twenty feet down into the midst of that seething, frothing, murderous maelstrom. "Jim, I'll do it first," he said. "But you have to do it after me." He flung himself into space and disappeared under tons of savagely rushing water and popped up a hundred yards downstream, waving his fist and screeching, "It's great! *Jump*!"

What could I do? I jumped.

Thirty miles down the Rokel River was Erik's village, Mapaki. Erik's playground here was a jungled gorge where the river narrowed into ferociously fast rapids. Here he introduced whitewater rafting, without the raft. He would point out a few strategic rocks for you to bounce off of. Then you let your naked body be swept into the rapids behind Erik for three hundred yards of breathless, adrenaline-addled terror.

Naturally, Erik was keen on motorcycles. We couldn't ride our Hondas together on the twisting bush paths between our villages without Erik insisting upon a full-throttle motocross race. Such tests of speed ended with me crashing my bike into 1) a washed-out culvert bed, 2) a banana tree, and 3) a herd of cows. Erik lost occasionally, too, but without grace. Once, on a race to the Bumbuna Waterfall, he was roaring along in the lead when he rounded a corner and found a coconut palm fallen across the path. The bike crunched into the trunk; Erik and the pillion rider were spreadeagled in the dirt. Up raced Percy and Jon, laughing in triumph as they edged around the tree to take the lead. Erik arched his back and kicked Percy's bike squarely in the gas tank. This send the bike over the path's edge and twenty feet down a densely wooded cliff. Percy somersaulted down with the bike and walked funny for weeks.

Erik's farewell stunt in Sierra Leone came just before the four of us were to leave on a motorcycle trip across Africa. This was Erik's last day in his village and we were waiting for him in a bar in a town called Maburka, five miles downriver. There is a narrow two-lane bridge that spans the Rokol here and a hundred feet below you can see, amid half-submerged boulders, the rusting wrecks of a score of trucks and cars that had tumbled off the bridge.

Erik walked into the bar with the new Peace Corps kid who was replacing him in Mapaki. Both were sopping wet. Why?

"Well, Jim," Erik said sheepishly. "I jumped off the Maburka Bridge."

"Erik ... why?"

"Well, I've always wanted to jump off the Maburka Bridge and this was my last chance, so ..."

"Perfect logic," Percy muttered in despair.

"Did you jump off, too?" I asked the new kid.

"Um, yeah. See, Erik said, 'I'll do it first—'"

"But you have to do it after me. I know, I know. Congratulations, kid. You're Sierra Leone's new Bull Goose Loony."

We took off across Africa aboard 175cc Honda Scramblers. Percy Brown got ninety miles outside the capital of Freetown when his rear tire suffered a blowout and he lost all his front teeth. We three survivors bashed on regardless.

When we got back to America, our biggest concern was how to get out of it again. Erik, a philosophy graduate, tried school again but academia, after Africa, seemed a mite tame. He set himself up as a carpenter in Colorado, installing door and window frames on new housing developments. He acquired an assistant and a pickup truck, but decided America was a mite tame too. So he re-enlisted in the Peace Corps in the Philippines to do the same thing he did in Africa: teach isolated hill tribes how to grow irrigated rice.

He sold everything he owned except the pickup truck and pointed it toward Manhattan where I was working as a Peace Corps recruiter. In Little Rock, Arkansas, he found Percy working in a shoe store.

"What're you doing, Percy?"

"Not much."

"Let's go to New York and see Jim."

"Okay."

In Wooster, Ohio, they found Jon working in a gas station.

"What're doing, Jon?"

"Not much."

"Let's go to New York and see Jim."

"*Okay*!"

The three of them turned up at my tenement on the Lower East Side at three in the morning. I had three squalid rooms, bathtub in the kitchen, pull-box toilet. They were delighted. We smoked, drank, laughed ourselves witless till way past dawn.

Erik was swiftly shacked up with an old friend named Alison. She was a fellow Zonian, tall, blond, willowy, with a mad gleam in her droopy blue eyes. I had a girlfriend at the time too, Fran Goldfarb, a sexually voracious but typically neurotic New York Jew who spent half her salary on shrinks. But her one redeeming quirk was that she loved horses and would take me up to a Catskills stable for two-hour gallops through the countryside.

We all agreed now that it would be a great idea to go horseback riding. Erik suggested a sporting twist: we'd do it while tripping on high-powered blotter acid. Alison had the acid. We gathered at her high-ceilinged flat on East 20th Street on the morning of my birthday. Alison had us all drink a concoction of powdered marijuana in honey for purposes of stamina, then distributed the little blotter tabs on our tongues like Communion.

We burst outside into the autumn sun and climbed into the pickup truck. There were still hippies in 1972 and we were a motley collection of beards, long hair, Fu Manchu mustaches, Percy and I in knee-length *ronka* robes, Erik sporting an locomotive engineer's cap, Percy a Fidel Castro campaign hat ... We were the height of freak chic.

Rocketing along the FDR drive, a pleasant roar suddenly came to our ears, the East River erupted into a million merrily dancing points of light, the colors lifted off the cars behind us and shimmered madly – crimson, shamrock green, robin's egg blue, banana yellow – and as the pickup swerved along the riverside curves, we three slammed into each other in the cargo bed, giddy as kids on a rollercoaster. We were inveterate dope smokers – hell, in Sierra Leone you could buy a shoebox full of the stuff for a dollar – but we had never felt such a ripping great high. This was *wonderful*. We were virgins and this was sex.

"Ooooh boy!" Jon said.

"Ooooh boy!" I said.

"Ooooh boy!" Percy said. "OboyOboyOboyOboy!"

Onward we soared, faster and faster, higher and higher. On the New York Thruway, we broke out into the countryside. Meadows undulated and swelled, farmhouses shimmered, forests in their autumn glory were a blazing symphony of color. On and on the phantasmagoric panorama rolled, scrolling out in ecstatic throbbing light.

This was bliss, unimaginable, unlimited, eternal ...

Eternal? How much longer could this go on?

Behind us were Mom and Pop cars, kids in the back seat. The parents glowered at us hippies, the kids smiled and flashed peace signs. We smiled and flashed back.

"You know what's funny?" Percy said. "We are so lost. And Erik is *driving*!"

We craned our necks around to see, through the cab window, Erik grinning at the wheel, Alison, next to him, gesticulating wildly, Fran looking out the passenger window. We would later learn that we were lucky to have Fran. Sober Fran was our Control. Erik was perfectly capable of driving the truck but at the toll stations he had no idea what those green papers and round pieces of metal signified. Fran briskly took charge.

There was no way of telling how long we were on the road. If we'd had watches, we'd have stared dumbly at these strange circular objects strapped to our wrists. But one thing was certain: we were cold. Percy had the worst of it. There was only room enough for two in the bottom of the truck bed. Percy, sprawled on top of us, was exposed to the wind.

"I'm cold," he whimpered. "I'm so cold."

Tears were streaking down his black cheeks, the salt drying white, cracking into rivulets, and this pathetic black wrinkled lizard kept croaking, "I'm cold, I'm cold."

I took charge. "Jon, let the lizard get down here in the bottom and you get up."

"What lizard?"

"Percy. Take his place."

"Balderdash."

"Just let him warm up a minute."

"No, it's cold up there."

"Just for a few minutes. Pity poor Percy."

"Pity poor Percy," Percy agreed.

"Then I'll be cold and I don't want to be cold," Jon said. "Let *him* be cold,"

"Aw, c'mon. How about I give you a good reason?"

"Wut?"

"It's my birthday."

"Oh," Jon reasoned. "Okay!"

But soon we were all cold and banged on the cab roof for Erik to stop. He pulled off onto a grassy shoulder and we tumbled out of the truck like clowns in a circus car. We whirled around drunkenly, waving our arms, shrieking with laughter and – was this our imagination? – traffic was slowing on the Thruway to gape at us. Look at the hippies!

We decided to get off at the next exit and find hot coffee.

Whatever the name of the town, it was typical Americana: white clapboard houses, big porches, tall shade trees. Erik pulled to a stop in a deserted street. We tumbled out of the truck again to play with the ankle-deep dead leaves. If anyone had seen us, they would have definitely decided something was wrong: grown men and women sitting in the middle of the street, hooting and laughing as they threw leaves in the air. Jon had the inspiration to reach into his pocket and toss green papers into the air as well. I couldn't have explained why but I knew this was wrong. So I picked them up and stuffed them in my own pocket.

Back in the truck and off to an old diner. Inside, the air was hot and steamy and the counter full. A waitress pointed us downstairs to a basement dining room. The walls were a throbbing blood red. We were mercifully alone as we waited for our coffee. Fran produced a bag of cookies and scattered them around the table. Percy was babbling incoherently about the walls closing in, about blood and Flash Gordon and the torture chamber of Ming the Merciless.

Fran impatiently tossed a couple of cookies at him. "Eat your cookies," she ordered.

"No. NO! I don't want your goddamn cookies!" Percy reared to his feet and backed away in horror and rage.

Just then the waitress came down the stairs with a tray of steaming coffee cups and came face to face with a raving black man with a badly scarred face and Fidel Castro hat and weird knee-length robe, mouth agape and eyes bulging with indignation. "No cookies for me, you conniving bitch!"

I felt soothing words were called for.

"Percy, sit down," I said.

"Why? WHY?"

"Eat your cookies. It's my birthday."

"Oh ... Okay."

Fran handled the bill and a big tip for the terrified waitress. As we finally escaped the diner, a customer at the counter muttered, "And *stay* the fuck out."

We needed privacy. Erik drove us out of town and down a dirt road out to a meadow surrounded by forest. He and Alison, Fran and I, slumped to the ground. Percy and Jon wandered off, heads thrown back to the sky, hands flying, raving happily.

The sun was setting and out of it flew rank upon rank upon rank of flaming chariots drawn by flaming horses and driven by flaming charioteers cracking flaming whips ...

Percy and Jon were hallucinating simultaneously, marvelling as fully-rigged white clipper ships sailed across the sky. Erik slapped the earth, crying joyfully, "Can't you see it *breath*? The whole planet's breathing!"

Percy and Jon returned, wild-eyed and raving like Old Testament prophets. As it was getting dark, I thought I might round up the troops.

"We're really gonna have to find a motel," I told Erik.

Back into the truck. Alison wanted to ride in the back, so I climbed into the cab with Erik and Fran. Now Fran was feeling a mite left out of things, what with all this talk of flaming chariots and clipper ships and respirating earth, and as we were driving through an overarching grove of trees, she exclaimed, "Isn't this just like a womb? Like we're entering a womb?"

Erik's eyes bulged and his fists tightened on the wheel. "WHAT?"

"No, Erik, it's not a womb," I assured him. "Just a bunch of trees."

"Oh ... Whew! Thanks."

Back in civilization, it was like a Peter Max cartoon, little toy cars bubbling down the road. Erik swung across traffic and into a motel parking lot. He had done well, I thought. Now I had to do my bit.

I strode manfully into the motel office and confronted the walrus behind the reception desk. The beast was three-hundred pounds with bristling whiskers and yellowing tusks. I ordered up two adjoining rooms for four men and two women, paid what I thought was an outrageously high bill, grabbed the keys.

"Whatever you do in there," growled the walrus, "clean up after you're done."

"Hey, we all have jobs," I protested weakly and fled out of the door.

The keys worked and suddenly we were behind closed doors, safe and warm. Fran went out and came back with coffee and sandwiches. Jon chomped into one, chewed violently with a dry mouth, and spat out breadcrumbs and lettuce: "This is a mattress sandwich!"

We turned on the television: Gary Cooper in *High Noon*. Things were settling down except the commercials would send Percy into a towering rage over their imbecility. Erik, restless as ever, went outside and came back to report that there was a bar attached to the hotel. Everyone trooped out for beer except for Fran and me who stayed in bed.

Fran was talking about marriage and our own house with – would you believe it? – a white picket fence. I stared at the beak of her nose and suddenly she was a featherless bird chirping nonsense. I can't marry a bird. Or maybe I could, if I cut off her beak. I did that with chickens in Africa.

Erik came back and roused us out the door. The walrus was behind the bar listening to a very voluble Percy. Jon and Alison were dancing to the jukebox. We went through a huge amount of beer very quickly and when the walrus closed the bar he said this was the best night he'd had since he opened the place. He was still curious about the four of us hippie guys and, you know, only two girls.

We brought long-necked Buds back to our rooms. I got back in bed with Fran. Erik took a shower with Alison, who invited Percy and Jon to join them. From the open bathroom door came squeals and giggles of delight. When they emerged naked, Alison got in bed with Jon. Now this was bad. This was against The Code.

Jon kept trying to have an intelligent conversation

with Erik while Alison manipulated him under the sheets. Erik listened with an embarrassed smile. Somehow, with grace, Jon kept his virtue, and Alison skipped off to sleep with Erik.

The next morning, we found a Howard Johnson's and ordered up a huge breakfast. But we were in no condition to eat it. Weary and shaken, we stared glumly at the uneaten food.

"*Gosh*!" I squealed. "Thanks, boys and girls! That was the swellest birthday party *ever*!

We roared.

I called in sick that day. In my office the next morning, the black girl at the desk behind me was wearing a bright multi-colored striped sweater that suddenly began undulating and shimmering ... But that was my only flashback. I never took acid again but treasure that one time I did. The lesson was that in a cold hostile world we were a band of brothers. Within a year, we had all escaped back to the tropics: Erik to the Philippines, Percy back to Sierra Leone, Jon to Mexico, me to Brazil. Our acid trip had taught us: always stay a moving target.

– 2 –

Erik wrote letters when he was drunk and stoned, always

on yellow legal notepaper in a large loopy scrawl replete with multiple dashes, exclamation points and abrupt changes of subject – speed freak style.

One of them reached me in Kilometer 46, forty-six kilometers west from the nearly town Altamira (Alta Lama, Alta Merde – high mud, high shit), which Time magazine had called "a tropical Dodge City" on the banks of the Rio Xingu, eight hundred miles from anywhere, where I was just finishing up planting sugar cane plots for a Brazilian research agency. I GOT THE BOAT, the letter opened.

When I stepped onto the tarmac at Manila Airport, Erik was on the observation deck, bearded and long-haired, jumping up and down and screeching in Timne, "*Sekke! Sekke nu! Tope an deera?*"

"*A yanke me der,*" I replied. I'm fine.

Erik got the boat when he met Dave Winslow, a local USAID honcho, who needed crew to sail his brand new yacht from a Bangkok boatyard to the Manila Yacht Club. Christened *Quetzal*, she was a thirty-foot ferrocement gaff-rigged cutter, a double-ender built along the lines of a Norwegian lifeboat. Not much for style or speed, but ideal for crossing oceans.

Winslow and Erik two-handed the boat down the Gulf of Thailand, around South Vietnam and two thousand miles later had reached the mouth of Manila harbor when a tropical gale tore away their mast. Shortly after they were towed into the yacht basin, Winslow got even worse news. USAID had transferred him from Manila to Niamey, Niger. Straddling the top of Nigeria, Niger is a half-million square miles of hot sand. Yes, smack plunk in the middle of the Sahara. Scant use for a sailboat.

Undaunted, Winslow hired Erik to refit the boat for him and sail it down the South China Sea, across the Indian Ocean, around the Cape of Good Hope and up to Lagos – halfway around the world.

My first sight of the *Quetzal* came as Erik rowed me out in his dinghy amid the gleaming sloops and schooners of the Manila Yacht Club. The wealthy owners employed live-in "boat boys" whose sole job was to keep teak and brass fittings in perfect sparkle. Erik was the only white boat boy and the *Quetzel* the Yacht Club's only eyesore. Dismasted still, she squatted at her mooring, cement hull pockmarked and streaked with rust, deck aclutter with paint buckets, mops, tools, rubber tires, pots and pans, broken funnels, stray shackles. From a laundry line astern flapped Erik's tattered underwear, soccer socks and Thai fisherman's pants.

"What do you think?" he asked doubtfully.

"Gorgeous!"

I meant it. She was thirty foot long, she floated, and she was *ours*. Belowdecks was a galley, two-berth salon with fold-up table, a toilet used only for storage, a forepeak with two more berths. Plus an icebox for beer, lockers crammed with canned goods, a well-stocked paperback library. What more could anyone want?

We passed the next six weeks making the *Quetzal* seaworthy. We stepped a new mast, rerigged the sails, sanded and varnished every inch of teak, chiselled out the rust in the hull, plugged the gaps with fresh cement. In our labors we were aided by the Beautiful Busty Barratella Sisters. We had met these two very rich Cuban American sisters at a folksinging bar where I would occasionally pick up a guitar and cadge for free beers. We lured them out to our boat and later, as martial law curfew hour loomed, taxied across town to their mansion in Makati. The family had gone to bed so we had the living room stereo to ourselves. As Dylan's new *Blood on the Tracks* played full bore, we were guzzling goblets of Chivas Regal and lying intertwined on the rug in an amorous heap when the door opened and there stood Mr Barratella himself, clad in a silk bathrobe and wielding an enormous samurai sword. His eyes bulged: his virginal daughters in the filthy clutches of two long-haired bearded degenerates! I leapt to my feet and approached him in a mendicant crouch. "Mr Barratella, sir," I squeaked. "Let me assure you that we are perfectly harmless."

After many soothing words from the two sisters, the ogre departed. We subsided into a confused embrace again. The older sister, nineteen, black-haired and tan, looked like Ali MacGraw. The younger, seventeen and heavy-set, was the smart and funny one, though suffering from a teenage infatuation with Ayn Rand. With the Marcos military curfew, we had no choice but to spend the night – Erik with Ali MacGraw, me with Ayn Rand – sneaking out of their beds scant hours before breakfast to greet the family with beaming innocent smiles. Over the next month the Beautiful Busty Barratella Sisters spent most nights on our boat, always pleading to the father the curfew excuse.

- 3 -

A misty morning of March 20, 1975, we weighed anchor, hauled up the mainsail, started up the small auxiliary engine and chugged out of the yacht basin, on our way to Africa. The engine gave out somewhere around Corregidor. All efforts at resuscitation failed; for the rest of the voyage the engine functioned purely as ballast. We had no radio, no RDF, no electricity even. We had a sextant on board, but never did figure out how to use it. Pure sailing by the seat of your pants. We did have charts and a hand-held compass, and set our course for Borneo, seven hundred miles south. Borneo's a pretty big island and we figured it would be hard to miss.

As evening fell, we moved into the great rolling swells of the South China Sea. Our hearty captain promptly became seasick. Mercifully, the night was clear and the wind steady and I had no problem keeping us on course till morning and Erik's revival. The operations involved in sailing the *Quetzal* were simplicity itself. There was the mainsail and the topsail above the gaff, and before the mast three headsails: stay, jib and flying jib. A knowledge of two hitches and a pair of callused palms were all that was needed to haul sail up or pull it down. Similarly, steering meant pushing the tiller in the direction you didn't want to go. Each of us spent twelve hours a day at the tiller. We wore only shorts, or nothing at all, and were soon tanned as dark as Malay fishermen.

The next two weeks were pure glamor: blue water and blue skies with only the occasional rainsquall. We had a good beam wind and as the boat stayed canted over to starboard, we learned to live atilt, using gravity and controlled falls and strategic handholds to clamber fore and aft. Dolphins often came up to frolic in our bow waves. Once, bouncing about on the bowsprit, I reached down and touched the dorsal fin of an unsuspecting dolphin, who rolled over to regard me with an intelligent eye for an instant before skittering away to the depths, frisky as a pup.

Best of all were nights alone at the tiller under a million stars, canted over and scudding along nicely, no sounds but the whoosh of water along the hull, bowsprit pointed at a star and the light of a full moon making the sails gleam like white satin. You would sing and pray and talk to yourself, unencumbered by memories or worries, alive solely for the moment.

On the fourth morning out we raised sight of Palawan. For two hundred miles we followed its coast of mountain and jungle before heading out to open sea. Three more days and the mountains of Sabah loomed up on the horizon. We sighted Jesselton with its great shining mosque and pushed on for another eighty miles to Labuan, where we tied up at the pier and passed the next three days in generally drunken and undignified behavior. April 10 we were off again, headed for Singapore, nine hundred miles to the west. The mountains of northern Borneo – so steep and wild and utterly desolate – might as well have been the Mountains of the Moon. It was no place to get shipwrecked. Which is what almost happened five days later.

We had passed the flaming gas rigs of Brunei, gone out of sight of land for a couple days and then returned to the coast, running with all five sails up to catch a stiff land breeze off the mountains, when the wind suddenly turned around out at sea, came roaring back and walloped us. In an instant we were knocked down.

"Knocked down" is a yachtsman's term for what happens in a bathtub when you blow too hard on your toy sailboat: it flops flat on its side.

A hellish racket sounded in the cabin as all our gear flew through the air and slammed against the port bulkhead. A wall of blinding rain crashed over us; water flooded the cockpit; a gale-force wind shrieked through the rigging. The boat was upended on its beam – one stiff wave would roll us over! With a flashlight jammed in my teeth I was sprawled amidships fumbling desperately with the topsail lines. Erik flew for the mast to haul down the main. In pitch darkness and freezing rain, warm seawater tugging at our knees, we worked frantically to free the tightly coiled lines. Erik got the main down and the boat lifted slightly. In an adrenaline frenzy I scurried forward for the staysail, Erik got the jib and at the end, with Erik straddling the bucking bowsprit and snatching down the flying jib while I yanked the wet nylon on to the foredeck, the boat was yawing and pitching wildly but upright – we weren't going to drown – and I spat out my flashlight in an hysterical Porky Pig imitation: "Tuh-tuh-tuh-tuh-tuh-tuh-that's all, folks!"

We put down anchors fore and aft and went below into the shambles of our cabin to break open a cask of fifty-year-old Filipino rum. The storm abated and, amazingly, within an hour the sea was flat and the sky tranquil with stars. Samba music blared from the cassette player; two gibbering gringos reeled about on deck, ecstatically grateful for the gift of life. There was an eerie green phosphorescence in the water and naturally Erik had to play with it, diving off the bowsprit and hauling himself down twenty feet on the anchor chain. I joined him down there and the two of us became flaming green figures in the world of black – a pair of incandescent astronauts out on a space walk.

33

For the next few days, though, we sailed in a subdued mood. That sea out there could kill you! Cloudy nights were agonizing because you couldn't see what was coming at you and every stray gust of wind had you flinching and nervously contemplating taking down more sail. After four days of being whipsawed by squalls and drizzle, we reached the northwest point of Borneo, St. Petrus Island. We were becalmed for two more days and a night. Across four hundred miles of open sea lay Singapore.

The wind finally picked up and we were off on the final leg. Midway to Singapore we anchored off a deserted island called Mendarik, harvested some coconuts, had a cookout on the beach and snorkelled along the coral reef where I saw, ten feet below, a sea turtle as wide as my outstretched arm. I dove down to say hello, but that turtle didn't get to be that big by being stupid. One look at me and he was gone.

On April 30, nearly six weeks out of Manila, we entered the Singapore Strait and passed the Horseborough Light. Twenty-five miles ahead we could see the glow from downtown Singapore. Monster supertankers lumbered all about us; we bobbed like a cork in their wakes. After a becalmed afternoon, an evening wind and current swept us through a maze of anchored shipping and right into the city. We anchored off Clifford Pier. Next morning when we went ashore we learned that Saigon had just fallen.

SINGAPORE GIRL

Part One

There's no sense in hating someone for not loving you, Jim reflects as he walks in the afternoon sunlight down a Singapore street, having left his hotel in search of food. No, not when there was nothing she could be but be who she is and nothing she could do but hurt and disappoint you who had no right to demand her to be who she was not nor could ever be nor, perhaps, could anyone be whom you insist on constructing your dreams upon. So he is left, once again, with himself. Someone, Jessie, said he looked eighteen and possessed by love he had felt eighteen and no doubt acted like a damn fool eighteen too. Scorned now, he's restored to his old self, ten years older, at his real age of twenty-eight, Jim, the old Jim, Diamond Jim, the drinker, guitar player, womanizer, and the sardonic laugh he directs to himself is suffused with the tired satisfaction of receiving yet another dollop of wisdom, the weary certainty that you cannot violate laws of the heart – that no woman who's not in love loves any man who openly professes to love her, who recklessly reveals his yearnings to her scrutiny, that to carelessly invest such esteem upon the listener makes her uncomfortable, unworthy of such attention and ultimately bored by it and so the one doing the loving is doubly deluded and ends up losing his would-be lover's respect. And that passions of the heart rarely endure voyages through space or passage through time.

So he should have known in Jakarta, did know in the cynical core of his being that languidly mocked his fervent religious sea-inspired visions, yet in faith still he said goodbye to his best friend and boarded a jet plane that in an hour and ten minutes returned him to where's he'd left by sail six weeks and four days before. Knowing in that same disbelieving core that he was going off half-cocked on another wild lurch of a dream only to collide inevitably into the cold grey brick of reality. That the Milly of his misted memory and frenzied future dreams did not exist, that the word itself Milly was nothing but an empty phonetic form, a random collection of Scrabble tiles, into which he poured all his life-long yearnings for love, home, stability, peace.

Spooning down his lonesome meal of duck and rice at a Chinese food stall, he is suddenly seized with the notion of writing down what happened, what really happened, and how he comes to find himself alone and anonymous in this city of 3 million, known only by one person who chooses not to know him any longer. So he now consigns to paper a weary confession that yes, with complete foreknowledge and full consent of the will, I have violated laws irrevocable, immutable and eternal as long as the human heart endures:

Love declared is loved scorned. Yes and passion endures until the rent is due. Yes and don't ever, ever, fall in love with a whore.

- 2 -

They had raised sight of Singapore after five weeks and 1,300 miles of sailing in the South China Sea, the great city at first but a strange glow on the horizon, unnatural brightness for eyes grown accustomed to nights at sea. It was an eerie evening of little wind, gaff creaking and sails flapping forlornly. There was no wind at all the next day as their sailboat drifted helplessly toward the palm trees and rusted tin roofs of a fishing village on the Malaysian mainland, and Jim had given it up for the night, was stoned and playing his guitar when a land breeze suddenly caught the sails and made them billow out nicely and the boat canted over and began with stately grace to glide forward. Slowly the towering buildings of Singapore began to take shape, their bright lights looming over red and green running lights of the moored ships at their feet. They took a sighting off the blinking green light of the

Fullerton Building and another red one further down the skyline and with a handheld compass triangulated their position.

Four hours later with Jim steering and Erik nervously keeping watch out on the bowsprit, they were dodging their way between the anchored freighters and tankers and supertankers to finally drop anchor a hundred yards from Clifford Pier, to smoke dope and drink Filipino rum till dawn in amazed celebration of having actually arrived where they had pointed the boat that misty morning six weeks before when they left Manila harbor.

They spent the next day drunk and a good part of the day after till well stoked up on grass they went out in a serious search for women. Their first childlike euphoria quickly dissipated into beery frustration and Jim bedded down with an old Chinese whore, paying her forty bucks for an all night deal but after the first dismal fuck, sick of her and disgusted with himself, he left her to wander the streets in the rain, heartsick for the flash and dance and warmth of the girls he'd known in Africa and Brazil.

His pent up want for women he channeled into writing, that feverish yearning for ecstasy he harnessed into a grand scheme of recollection, of recapturing the past, of tracing how his present rooting in Singapore had grown out of seeds sown in Africa four years before when he and Erik had sat naked and stoned before the Bumbuna waterfall and dreamed aloud their plans to sail a boat around the world, and earlier still, Erik as a kid in Panama, hanging out at the Balboa Yacht Club, sailing dinghies on day trips to the outer islands, listening to the tales of blue water sailors.

Now every morning Jim would rise at dawn to scrawl in silence and solitude, intent on weaving together the wild strands of fate that had brought them to Singapore, this first way-stop on a mystic waterborne return to Mother Africa. How in Monrovia and Accra they'd hung around docks and seamen's clubs and met up with a teenage fraternity of dinghy sailors in Lagos. How back in America at their first Peace Corps reunion in two wooden lakeshore shacks in Minnesota – running around in a daylight frenzy of fishing and water-skiing, volleyball and tetherball, and night revels stoked on Strohs and dope, skinny-dipping off the pier, admiring each other's wives and girlfriends in the moonlight – Erik suddenly turned serious and silenced the cackling tribe with a heartfelt speech about Nixon and Mitchell and how America was no place for free spirits, this was no longer our country, the walls were closing in, our only escape was back to the tropics.

Jim had reached some twelve thousand words when one hectic nearly windless afternoon they transferred the boat up the coast from Clifford Pier to the Oasis, a round Chinese restaurant-nightclub complex up on stilts in Katong, near the filthy estuary of the Kallang River.

43

To celebrate, Jim and Erik began drinking beer, joking, reminiscing, reveling in their present freedom, and they kept drinking till nightfall set them on another careening search for women. They lurched through bars down Arab Street, morosely gulping down beers, conversation desultory now, on the ancient sailors' search for women.

- 3 -

Out on the midnight street, darkness is the enemy, bright lights your only friend. Horny men are mothlike in their hunger for light and light attracted Jim and Erik down a side-street of ancient Chinese shophouses to turn a corner and find row upon row of tables occupied by hordes of white people sitting in front of bottles of beer and looking about expectantly. Realizing they were famished, Jim and Erik wolfed down heaping plates of fried rice and swilled more beer.

They arrived in two and threes parading down the aisles between the tables, outrageously made-up, coiffured in elaborately flowing wigs, dressed in blatant gaudy flamboyant fashions – flash silk hotpants, skimpy miniskirts, elegant evening gowns – teetering about on high platform shoes or mincing in long-sheathed boots. Brazen, blatant, wanton, flaunting their merchandise, out-thrust tits and wiggling ass and ruby lips and wildly arched eyebrows. Here a redhaired Malay girl in a flimsy green satin blouse half-opened and straining with the weight of her plump dark breasts, there a tall pale Chinese girl with enormous mascaraed eyes, miniskirted and meshstockinged, sashaying down the aisle, and there a tall dark husky Indian girl in a tight leaf-patterned silk catsuit that clings to every contour of her plump rollicking buttocks. A phantasmagorical parade of women flaunting their readiness to fuck, this tawdry, glittery, carnal spectacular pageant, this carnival of savage lust in staid Singapore.

Erik and Jim were sitting up in their chairs now, excited, ready to be entertained, ready for the show. "Christ!" Erik exclaimed. "It's like a wild far-out oriental imitation of whores in America. I mean they're putting on what they think whores should look like. It's like a fantastic parody of whores."

Parody indeed. Far more than they'd dreamed. For as far as the eye could see down the whole brightly lit narrow street, that doomed passageway of tables and white faces flushed red and drunk now howling and hideous in the spotlights, every whore who wiggled and gave coy inviting looks, laughed loudly or sat primly at a table or sauntered seductively down the aisle, each and everyone of those painted, wigged, tight-skirted whores held a secret curse tight between their legs. This was Bugis Street.

45

- 4 -

"I don't want to analyse my feelings for you," he said yesterday after they'd come off the beach and lay in the grass under the shade of palm trees, green fronds making shifting patterns against the blue sky.

"You have to," she said. "Don't you see, you have to."

In the long moments of silence he saw that his dream was empty, a vacuum that could never compel the flesh and blood, memories, desires and stubborn being of Milly Visweswaran to enter. She would not be his idol, not consent to simply be a romantic figment in Jim's imagination, and in a sudden harrowing realization he knew that yes there was a frightening lot to consider before he could speak again to that beautiful brown face fixed now so intently upon him. And all he could say was to make the sickeningly terrifying admission: "Yes, you're right. I do."

For he had long ceased to think of her as a boy, already his mind's eye had performed the castration the surgeon's knife had yet to accomplish. And, as woman, how could she fail to fall in love with him? To join the parade of black and white and brown bodies that had lain gratefully under him, squandered their love to him who was now under the delusion that he was giving love to her, to Milly.

He knew only a few fixed lights of her true identity, like

stars glimpsed at sea through the shifting passage of night clouds, while her true essence was concealed in galaxies upon galaxies invisible to Jim's myopic eye.

So now, finishing his second beer and ready to return to his hotel room, he does not forget.

"I just want to forget you," he told her this morning on the balcony of Jackie's house. But now he knows there is no forgetting. To forget Milly Visweswaran is to forget Jim Eckardt. Lost somewhere in the intergalactic mystery of her being is the hidden source of what Jim has spent too many savage years trying to flee – his very soul.

And the destination for these pages which he scribbles now in the fading light of day? Is this an exorcism or a tentative step to salvation?

– 5–

It began on Bugis Street – this uncharted doomed odyssey into self – with Jim lurching out of his chair in search of women. Erik, shy as always, remained seated with his beer and his observations, but Jim, ever randy and ready, plunged on through the parade of lost souls to the table where a lone whore was seated, thus inexorably fixing the course of his life.

Up close she was of course not all she had appeared

to be. Powder failed to mask the pockmarks, mascara to enchant those tired eyes. Her smile was as practiced as her conversation, questions – his name, where he was from – being framed in a surprisingly deep voice, a weary charade gamely carried on to barely conceal her utter indifference to him and the faceless legions of men before him. Jim's eye wandered to the next table, the beautiful redhaired Malay girl was watching him appraisingly, and the dark Indian girl with steeply arched penciled eyebrows framing deep-set black eyes unfathomable, languid lazy power in those black eyes that so magnified and made compelling her bright smile of invitation. Jim smiled back at her.

"You know what I am, don't you?" the whore at his table was saying.

"What? Excuse me?"

"You know that this is Bugis Street? That none of use are really ladies."

Jim, slack-jawed and open-mouthed, wide-eyed, feeling hot blood rush to his face.

"Have you ever had an experience with—"

"No. Never."

"You should try it. It's an experience."

He looked back at the Indian girl, her heavy brown breasts slung in a flowered green silk halter, smooth brown arms, long glossy black hair splayed about softly rounded knobs of her shoulders, siren call of those mystic black eyes, that great ruby slash of a mouth, pursed plump lips now blowing him a kiss – a man?

"An experience," the whore was saying. "Most men who come here have a very good time. I can show you a very good time."

"Excuse me," he said, rising from his chair, his legs suddenly weak, boneless. "I've got to think about it."

So he knew now as he recrossed the aisle back to where Erik sat innocently watching the show, knew irrevocably what Erik grinning, sipping his beer, was so oblivious to, that the show he was enjoying was the grandest and cruelest of deceptions, a tawdry bright illusion of tinsel and paint and elastic and mime, that the whores, these gaudy flamboyant strutting whores, were being impersonated by actors. Jim watched, swallowing his beer with difficulty, his heart beating thunderously, his breath forced and shallow, a weakness and trembling in his limbs, for now knowing of the terrible secret curse of all the performers before him, yet he still ached for the Indian girl, and when he saw her stand and saunter slowly into the drugstore behind her table, saw the telltale broadness of her shoulder blades now yet his gaze was trapped, mesmerized, fixed immutably upon the roll and sway of that sweet silky ass and he stood to cross the aisle again, this time with foreknowledge and trembling certainty, to pass inexorably among the tables of whores, oblivious to their looks and the looks of the surrounding white people redfaced now and boisterous from drink, on into the drugstore to lean next to her on the glass-topped counter and place a single white finger on her smooth brown forearm and say in a lust-choked voice, "Hi. What's your name?"

"Jackie," she replied.

– 6 –

In the darkness of the cab on the way to her place she kissed him fervently, then she cushioned her head against his chest and they rode in silence for a while, his arm around her board soft shoulders and his hand restlessly caressing the silken softness of her arm, breathing in the scent of her hair and perfume.

"You know what I am, don't you?" she asked him.

"Yes. Yes I do," he said, such knowledge rendered meaningless, denied by the stiff unbelief of his aching loins, helplessly drawn by this strange creature huddled under his arm, broad man's shoulders under his arm yet his palm cupped the pendulous softness of her breast, and his mind reeled with incredulity, the insane paradox, and he abandoned himself, let himself go, drifted, the surging wild tumult of his crazed lust growing swelling howling like a sea storm and he doomed, lost, drowning.

The cab stopped at a two-storied suburban house. Still unbelieving that he was going to do this thing as he followed her up the stairs to her room, watching her silk-clad bottom swaying above him, his whole body coiled and tensed with electric energy wired to the heady jolting erotic thrill of the forbidden, the bizarre, the unthought of, a weird giddy plunge into the unknown.

Naked then in her bed, she chided him for his beer belly, "You should take better care of yourself," as slowly she peeled off the green catsuit and stood revealed before him, her smooth brown body taking a glossy gleam from the dim dresser light, firm black-nippled breasts and long smooth thighs and black triangular bush with a tiny black G-string to keep her secret safe, and then smiling slightly, looking into his eyes, she lowered herself slowly, gracefully to the bed and lay down beside him. He threw his arms around her, hugging her in his lonely need and grateful for the feeling of her warm body pressed up to his and her strong arms hugging him back, his eyes closed and lips and teeth feeding off the scented nape of her neck, feel and smell of her hair covering his face with blessed oblivion, and for a long warm delicious moment he was not alone, no longer adrift at sea nor marooned on the long rocky island of his mind. She gave of her comfort, her breasts to suck, her arms holding him, her hands caressing, then murmuring "Let me go down on you" she took him slowly into her mouth, toying with him till he was writhing in mindless joy, not caring now, oblivious to Jackie's curse, surrendering himself to her gentle warm wet mischievous working lips and tongue. And then she stopped, looking at him with glazed, famished eyes, and saying "You've got a lovely cock. Come on, let's make love," suddenly frightening him, his mind's voice shouting *what am I doing?* and she on her back now, her legs spread for him, a white towel between her brown thighs, and now he was hovering over her muttering embarrassed "I don't know what to do," and she responding with a throaty chuckle seizing him suddenly in her hand and with a deft flick of the wrist shoving him up inside her. And in wild delight he languidly rolled his hips feeling himself churning inside her hot slick shelter, feeling warmth and safety and joy flood into every dim corner and crevice of his being, the sailor finally home from the sea.

- 7 -

They lay side by side afterwards, faces close together, noses almost touching, and talked of little things, made the little jokes lovers do once they have spent themselves loving. She told him that she and the Malay girl – Sarah – had both had their eyes on him and had decided to let the best girl win. She asked him why he had not gone off with the first girl he was with and he said simply, "She was not beautiful. You are." He told her something of who he was, how he had come to be in Singapore. She told him little about herself but she spoke intelligently, saying she knew who she was and was not ashamed of who she was, that she had a boyfriend, a Frenchman (whose cock, she informed him, was thicker than Jim's own). She seemed open and receptive to him, and Jim, calm now, relaxed in her presence, felt with a happy thrill that perhaps he had made a friend.

They made love again, fiercely, she biting his shoulder and raking her nails down his back and he, maddened, plunging and swooping and pounding into her, prolonging her anguished pleasure till he heard her wail, a long exhilarated shriek of joy, felt her stiffen and shudder beneath him and then he was lost soaring upward to a blinding pinnacle and poured himself out in savage oblivion.

Spent, sweat-slick, panting, they lay a long time, and then gradually returned to themselves. He raised his head from where it had been buried in the sweaty thicket of her hair, looked down into her face, brown and serene and beautiful, her great black eyes looking up at him with what woman's pain and ecstasy and wisdom he could never hope to know and bewildered he stared down into those black wells of her eyes till he could bear it no longer and cupping her face tight in his hands he pressed a hard kiss on her lips and her hands came up behind his neck to pull him down more urgently to her.

Shortly afterward she returned to her world, to Bugis

Street, left him alone with a bottle of beer and a *Playboy* magazine for company. She had smiled ruefully, patted his cheek and rolled away from him on the bed and he knew as sure as he had touched her that he had lost her now. For sex with a client while sometimes pleasurable is never real, never as real as Bugis Street. She sat in front of her dressing table, brushing her wig, chatting amiably, telling him she needed money and was going back to Bugis Street for one more trick and he did not mind, did he? Would he please understand?

- 8 -

For Jackie, for Milly, for the whole misbegotten tribe of Bugis Street, they had eschewed the evidence of their bodies, rejected what mother and father had fashioned, ignored the fierce demands of family and school and church, endured ridicule and malice to follow with unswerving determination and stubbornness and courage what only their puny women's hearts decreed, to deny what society and their own absurd genitals posited. No, they are not men and maleness was to be hated and ruthlessly crushed in them.

So in some part of their being they could not help but hate men, even as women they longed to be dominated and fucked by that very stiff uncompromising maleness they had foresworn. Whoredom came naturally to them. To regard men as cocks, differing only in shape and size and proficiency. They could manipulate and create the most excruciating embarrassments for their would-be lovers simply because beyond as cocks and sources of money, men as individuals did not interest them. Their real interest and abiding love lay not in any man but in the woman's image that stared back at them so beautifully from their dressing table mirror. Their real eternal love was the reflected image of themselves, their consuming passion reserved only for the mirror image of illusion, makeup, costume and pose, eternal theater with actress and spectator the same person, an endless drama on a private stage played out in the bottomless narcissistic pools of mirror time.

So Jim, waiting for Jackie's return that rainy night should not have been surprised when she appeared at the bedroom door with another man in tow, and in garbled explanation consigned him (Jim) to a cot next to the bed.

He lay in agony on his back with his arm planted over his eyes staring out wildly into a prison of black, listening in outraged horror at the sounds of their lovemaking, still wanting Jackie and loath to get up, storm out, leave the first and only kind person who gave him some comfort, yet feeling sordid, bitterly humiliated, wanting her so badly he finally took her on the bed while the other man watched and even reached out once to stroke Jim's pumping back till Jim swung his arm out and shoved him violently back to the far side of the bed. And afterward he was ashamed. He could accept the G-string and the white towel but he'd be damned if he'd stand to have some faggot watch, and when Jackie left for the bathroom he told the man flatly to leave and, cowed, the man acquiesced, only to have Jackie return and convince him to stay. So utterly defeated, Jim pulled on his jeans muttering, "This sure is a tough town for dumb gringos."

Yet Jackie was not unkind. She called a taxi for him, promised to meet him the next day at the Lido for a movie, and stood in his arms by the staircase. "Please understand me," she said. "He's a steady customer and I need the money."

"Okay, okay. I just wish you didn't have to do it."

"What else can I do? I can't help being what I am. It's not my fault. Please understand. I have no other way to live."

Before he left she took his face in her hands and kissed him gently and stood back to look at him and ask, "Are you okay?"

- 9 -

"Are you okay?"

How many times would he come to hear these three words from Milly? Repeated over and over with an expression of solicitude whether real or feigned he would never know. Did she adopt the phrase from Jackie or teach it to her? Or was it perhaps part of the standard lexicon of whores – part of the care and handling of customers? A crafty show of concern to tame the raging male ego.

Whatever the origins of the phrase it would be wrong to say that Jackie and Milly never meant it, that their compassion and kindness were not often very real. Manipulating men was their work. Yet the best of the Bugis Street tribe, and Jackie and Milly were among the very best, had through sheer indomitable will and natural God-given grace transcended their bodies to achieve a womanhood whole and complete and separate from their night-time work as whores.

So was it that they were really women as they insisted, that whoring was a job they engaged only under dire economic necessity? Or did whoring fulfill a deep need in them, the act of flaunting, performing, parading down Bugis Street, with such an appreciative audience of drunken white faces, the thrill of conquest, snaring night after night men dazzled and drawn mothlike to their incandescent femininity? Proof again and again that yes they are desired by men, yes they are women, with only age to put an end to their starring role as eternal female.

Yet grant them that they are truly women, that they

require only the surgeon's skillful scalpel to right the hoax played on them by nature. Perhaps their curse lays deeper, in their narrow minds and battered feelings and hardened hearts, the tragic result of the pitiless years of lonely adolescent struggle and the years more of living on the outlaw fringe, the nether world of Bugis Street, the cramped purlieus of whores and customers, of knowing and trusting only their own kind banded together for protection against the hostile mocking world, a beleaguered lost tribe. They are survivors, weary spent damaged dazed and forever incapable of being warm spontaneous loving women. They have known too many men and believe in none. What wellsprings of innocence they once possessed have long since dried up, leaving them incapable of belief or acceptance or understanding or love of men.

Perhaps this is their real curse and painful doom.

- 10 -

Having gone out to the boat briefly and given Erik the *Playboy* and replied "Fantastic" to the inevitable question of how she was (as undoubtedly Jackie was called upon by Sarah to report how Jim had been), Jim stood Saturday noon in front of the Lido waiting for Jackie. He waited for an hour till she showed up, wearing a red blouse and tight white jeans.

Her face was garishly made up and in the harsh light of day there was something undoubtedly false about her. As they walked together down Orchard Road, people passing on the sidewalk seemed to look strangely at her, and Jim walked at her side in constrained silence as she prattled on about how sorry she was late and no she's couldn't spend any more time with him today as she had an old Englishman, a steady customer, to take care of but she would have the old guy drive him to Changi and drop him off at her sister's house, you'd like to meet my sister, wouldn't you?

Too weary to be disappointed, he agreed. Sure, he'd like to meet her sister. What better thing did he have to do today?

The Englishman had a white goatee and an air-conditioned BMW and drove Jim and Jackie to Changi making forced casual conversation till they pulled up at 5 Jalan Meragi. Jackie rang the bell and there stood Milly draped in a white bath towel. Seeing the two male strangers, she squealed in embarrassment, doing a dancing jig step backwards and then running off on dark bony coltish legs to the kitchen. When she reappeared, clad in a white blouse and an old red skirt, she gave them Coca Colas and asked Jim if he was hungry.

"I'm starving."

"I only have rice and, you know, native food."

"Native food is fine."

When Jackie and the Englishman left (Jackie giving Jim a kiss on the cheek and a furtive tweak to his crotch), Milly went to the kitchen to heat Jim's food while he sat at a dining table, sipping a Coke, smoking a cigarette, and wondering if Milly was really a sister. When she came out with his food he studied her face. She was a younger, smaller, more delicate version of Jackie. His scrutiny was obvious for she asked, "What are you looking at?"

"Sorry. You look so much like your sister. Except you're prettier. Your bones are finer, the bones of your face, your cheekbones are more delicate." But his first real judgement he reserved for himself: a certain thickness to her neck, a heaviness in her jaw warned him that he had not left Bugis Street.

But she was beautiful, of dainty and gentle movement, of a slow stately grace, putting him in mind of Dylan's song:

"I once loved a girl, her skin it was bronze

With the innocence of a lamb, she was gentle as a fawn."

How innocent she was he would come to know. But gentle she surely was, her every movement and gesture invested with a fawn's alert tentative shy grace.

She sat and smoked a cigarette as he ate nervously and answered her questions. He told her he had been with Jackie the night before.

"You have been to Bugis Street?" she asked him.

"Yes. Last night. It was my first time. My first experience."

"I'm sorry about the food. It's only native food. I hope it's not too spicy for you."

"No, it's delicious. I like spicy food. I lived three years in West Africa and people there use a lot of red pepper. I got to like it."

"Would you like a joint?"

"Joint? Dope? Sure."

"Here, you can roll it while I'm taking a shower. Or do you want to smoke it now?"

"No, after you shower. And you roll. I'm terrible at it."

Later then he lay on her bed and watched fascinated as her long nimble brown fingers fashioned an absolutely perfect joint. She'd slipped a Neil Diamond tape into the bedside cassette player, then sat on the floor, draped in a white bath towel, her hair wet and falling free about her shoulders. She handed him the joint to light.

Holding his breath in, he passed the joint back to her, watching her hand as she took it, a large hand, well-formed, long slender fingers with bright pink nails. Back and forth the joint went as Neil Diamond sang, "I was lonely and she was lonely …"

Time slowed, then vanished. Milly gazed raptly at the joint's burning ember glowing in the near dark room, and

61

before Jim in timeless glory and serene splendor surged a luminous vision of the eternal girl-child chastely wrapped in white baring her arms slender and brown and her hair a shiny tangled black cascade tumbling free about her shoulders and in a sudden enthralling moment of wonder her eyes moved from rapt contemplation of the burning ember, rose slowly and met his own gaze and she waiting still and speechless poised below him, and she smiled at him, a dazzling white smile of such radiant beauty that he felt tears spring to his eyes. He lowered his gaze, fixing his vision on the tiny orange glow that lay nestled between her fingers and after an infinity of voyaging through the convoluted inner spaces of his mind, his heart throbbing with rapture and his nerves stretched taut to the snapping point, he watched dumbly as the orange light moved insistently towards him, the joint, she was offering him back the joint. Slowly he reached out both hands. With his left he plucked the joint from her fingertips and with the right he clasped her empty hand. She squeezed back and laughed and he laughed too, suddenly liberated, the strange spell broken. He put the joint to his lips and took a long hungry toke.

"And I was lonely and she was lonely ..."

He turned her hand over looking into her white palm crazily crosshatched with a myriad profusion of lines, an old woman's palm.

"How old are you?" he asked her.

"Twenty-one. How old are you?"

"Twenty-five," he lied, feeling no guilt if thinking him younger she would like him the more. It seemed too much to hope that this slender radiant beauty could like him. And suddenly from somewhere he drew up the courage to look her in the face, seeing the delicate cheekbones and soft round contours of her cheeks, the plump curve of her lips. She was intent on fastening the joint to a roach clip. He slid down off the bed on to the floor beside her. She looked up and smiled at him. He watcher his hand move with agonizing slowness to rest on her smooth warm cheek. With a sinuous feline motion, she rubbed her cheek against his hand, closing her eyes, and after some moments of silence she said, "Jim, you know I'm a working girl."

"Sure. Money's no problem."

"I mean I hope you don't mind. It sounds awful."

"Don't even think about it, Milly. Milly, you're so beautiful."

She took a long deep breath, looking at him, and a slow small smile came to her lips and she leaned forward slowly, ever so slowly, her face looming before him closer and closer and he not moving, watching wide-eyed as her face swelled in beauty before him to obliterate all vision and her lips touched his.

- 11 -

At sundown, barefoot, sandals in hand, they strolled down
the line of surf at Changi beach. Hands linked, they walked
in serene silence, their feet slapping in rhythm on the cool
wet sand.

"How do you feel?" she asked him.

"Happy."

"Is that why you're so silent?"

"Yes. How do you feel, baby?"

"Happy. I'm happy."

The sun was low on the calm rippling water and the
western sky was filled with triple-tiered tumbling clouds, a
magnificent pageant of bright yellow, orange, pink, blazing
crimson. Jim watched a tan-sailed fishing skiff heading for
shore, tacking against a land breeze. He was happy, at
peace, his heart stilled with tenderness and contentment.
And it was not the sea this time that provoked his happiness
and not, as in the past, green African mountains and waterfalls, or the Amazon jungle at sunset, or the speed of motorcycles and sailboats, but simply a girl, this strange skinny
dark Indian girl, this lovely stranger whose hand he held,
who hours before had been straddled on top of him, locked
with him in a pounding dizzy-driven frenzy of love.

Would she stay by him? Would she come to reveal
herself to him, shed light on her dark mystery, narrate the

joys and sorrows of her past, and tell him of her dreams? These questions were not anxious ones for he was satisfied to simply hold her hand and share with her this sunset and the sea and the evening breeze, content and at peace with the long present moment, the moment enough for him, the steady languid joy of walking with her at land's end and sea's beginning.

They ate chicken satay in a beachfront restaurant. He borrowed a guitar from a Malay kid and sang her a song, looking in her face and the sea and the sky behind her, exulting in his happy right and privilege to gaze into her eyes and sing,

"Woman of the country now I've found you,
Longing in your soft and fertile delta
And I whisper sighs to satisfy your longing
For the warmth and tender shelter of my body
And you're my – me oh my – delta lady
Yes you're my – me oh my – delta lady."

– 12 –

He was doomed to love her before he knew her, entranced by this curious self-possessed exquisite face, this smooth brown fine-boned face, and black limpid eyes he would lose himself staring into, black depthless pools he would tumble into helplessly, falling, sinking, oblivious, peacefully drowning. Seeing her the next morning as they stood together leaning on the roof of the launch chugging through the calm blue waters heading out of Changi and onward to an outer island, she under his arm, pressed up against his side, her thick unruly black hair blowing in the sea breeze, bright sunlight gleaming on the smooth mahogany of her features, her eyes squinted against the wind and her strong white teeth flashing in a happy laugh; and more, enthralled, held spellbound by her movements, a sublime serenity permeating her every motion as she cooked satay for him in leaf-dappled sunshine under the trees on the rim of the white sand beach on that enchanted island. In silent reverence he watched fascinated the meticulous way her delicate hands tended the brazier fire, turned the roasting barbecue sticks and arranged the sauce bowls, her feminine wholeness radiant in the grace and artistry with which she performed the small woman's tasks she set herself to. She was whole and complete unto herself, mindful of the fire and sizzling meat, going about things slowly with dignity and self-possession in a different time scheme from Jim the fast-talking American. She abided in an Asian eternal present, elemental, powerful, beyond his ken, a wonder and delight to behold.

The day was theirs alone, a bright luminous day of sunlight sparkling on the white sand and dancing in the blue waters. Milly running down to the beach, exuberant, laughing, untamed, plunging into the sea with a shriek of animal glee. Finally, far from Singapore, was she free? A free woman prancing on the sand, frolicking in the sea.

Jet planes passed overhead and Milly seemed to have an encyclopedic knowledge of airlines, making a merry game of identifying Qantas, Thai Airways, Air France, Garuda, Pan Am.

She seemed released from preoccupation with herself and her problems – the biggest being Derek, the British seaman and long-time live-in lover she was trying to liberate herself from – and for once forgetful of her appearance, no need now to anxiously ask "Do I look all right?" that constant plea for the reassuring "Yes, Milly, you're gorgeous," as she fussed and fidgeted in nervous preparation that morning to venture out into the public streets. She had told him how self-conscious she could be, how she dreaded public exposure and embarrassment.

Now she could simply be herself, free to enjoy sea and sky, hot sand and cool water, seabirds calling and palm fronds rustling in the wind.

So they strolled laughing down the beach, the beer-bellied gringo and the slender Indian girl, so utterly different yet delighted in their discovery of each other. Their individual pasts seemed to vanish in their present sharing of their own magical world. Jim, watching a big Singapore Airlines 747 passing overhead, asked her, "Have you ever been out of Singapore?"

"Only once. I went with Derek once on his ship to Vietnam."

"Would you like to travel, to know other countries?"

"Oh yes. I plan to leave Singapore."

"So one day, Milly, you'll be up there on one of the planes flying high and free."

But even on this island she could not be totally free from the shackles of her past. It was Jim's fault, prodding her with questions about her family. She told him of her mother and brothers and sisters, and how in the end they rejected and abandoned her.

"Even if they have never done anything for me in all these years, I still love them. I'll always love my mother even if—" Her voice cracked, broke, tears springing to her eyes. "But who wants a freak? A transex? What's going to happen to me?"

He clumsily took her into his arms, embracing her for what consolation he could give, silent, for there were no words he could say, holding her tightly until her sobbing ceased and she pushed him away with an embarrassed laugh.

- 13 -

Back home, Milly took a shower. She draped a gauzy scarf

around her hips and sashayed topless around the kitchen, preparing dinner. Afterward they played Scrabble, Milly squirming in excitement, cupping her breasts and thumbing her thick black nipples, leaving Jim dizzy with lust. After she beat him badly in the first game and he barely won the second, she insisted on a third game. Upstairs she told him to take a shower. When he came back to the bedroom, she was sound asleep.

Jim lay awake next to her knowing even this early, this second night in her bed, that this was no idle harbor romance.

He looked over at her sleeping form, heard the rhythmic rise and fall of her breathing, and he gazed upward into the darkness and prayed God that he would not hurt this girl.

He had hurt almost every girl who'd had the misfortune to know him. "A man always remembers his first love. The other tend to meld together," H.L. Mencken once wrote. And since he had lost his first love, Jim had yet to fail to humiliate and take advantage of every girl foolish enough to surrender herself to him. In Africa their names were Adama and Ola, and Yamansa and Sentu and Mabinti. In America, Aileen, Joyce, Susan. In Brazil, Edilsia, Rosa, Clarissa, Leide, Alda. In the Philippines Leta and Maggie. He had left the best ones crying – Adama, Edilsia, Aileen – not out of malice but from a ruthless determination to stay free, untrammeled by lover and home, a traveling man with but temporary use for women. He would never be serious about anyone, never settle down.

What would happen to Milly? God knows she had been hurt enough already.

Now as he lay in her bed, in her home so spotlessly clean and well ordered, he realized how tired he was, how bone-weary of traveling. He had spent too many savage years roaming, careening from continent to continent, orgasm to orgasm, grabbing pleasure where he found it, his only loyalty to speed and music and wild dancing and drunken carousal. He'd gone homeless too long, never realizing till this moment in Milly's bed how deeply he missed having a home.

That afternoon as Milly gathered twigs for the fire, she told him that there was a Tamil proverb that said a girl who knows how to make a fire would make a good housewife, and he had to agree that it was a dandy fire she'd made.

— 14 —

Next morning she sat at her dressing table for an hour preening herself before the mirror in preparation to go to the market. Jim, laying on her bed, watching her, wondered why she dallied so long before the mirror when she really used but little makeup. But he was just coming to know

Milly and was unaware of the more sinister motives that lurked behind her fascination with the mirror.

Jim was past his first overawed impression of her physical beauty, could look critically at her now, see the black marks on her legs, her over-plucked eyebrows, her miniscule breasts and bony shoulders. It was all part of getting close to her as a real person. He was slowly coming to know the history behind this girl, groping toward a sense of who she was.

On her dressing table was a framed studio portrait of Milly and her husky English sailor boyfriend Derek. Her breasts were much plumper in the photo. "I've lost weight," she admitted. "I've been under a lot of stress. I can't take him much longer."

She was talking now of Singapore's legal policy toward transsexuals, how at eighteen, with parents' consent, a sex change operation was provided free at a government hospital, or above twenty-one for S$2,000 at a private hospital.

"Would you like to have an operation like that?" he asked her.

She turned quickly from the mirror, looking intently at him and crying, "Yes! Oh yes! Oh Jim, there's nothing else I want in this world. If I could have my operation, I'd be the happiest girl in the world."

"And it costs two thousand. Singapore dollars?"

"Yes."

"Well, maybe I can help you," he said, letting the subject drop, with the guilty knowledge that he had the money to pay for her operation, could spare it easily to fulfil her lifelong dream. But having lost a couple thousand dollars in a Brazilian motorcycle deal just a few months before, he was wary of squandering his inheritance, and so he kept a prudent silence. He would want to know her a lot better before he revealed how rich he was. He felt something would be spoiled between them if she knew too soon.

In her conversation in the weeks to come she would return again and again to the only dream that mattered to her, the operation. She seemed to have little interest in dreams of love and none at all in plans for her future education, job, career. There was only the one abiding obsession in her life: to rid herself of the cruel joke nature had played on her. And she clung to the childish belief that following the operation she would find herself resurrected as a complete normal adult woman. But surgery does not change personality and in many ways Milly was very much a child, emotionally stunted, ever dependent upon men to provide her security and shelter, ever needful to be in some man's keep. She was self-absorbed, self-centered and self-deluded. It was difficult imagining Milly as an independent woman, taking a job, charting the course of her own life, expanding the reach of her mind and her talents.

But of these thoughts he was innocent that hot sunny

morning in May when they left the house and strolled hand-in-hand down the street on their way to market. Milly plucked a bud from a plant and told him that when she was in school they used them for water fights.

"Water fights? What do you mean?"

Laughing, she squeezed the bud and squirted a jet of water into his face.

"You miserable bitch. Gimme some of those things."

Shouting and laughing, they ran down the street shooting water at each other till Jim wagged the two-fingered peace sign at her in abject surrender.

The morning was hot and Jim had a raging thirst by the time they reached the market. They sat on stools at a corner drinks stand and Milly ordered them something called ice pudding. Jim, wrapping his parched lips around a straw, eagerly sucked up ice cold sweet coconut milk and fruit juice and thought he had never tasted anything so damn good.

In the market he followed Milly with the basket as she bargained with the vendors in Chinese, Malay, and Tamil, loading the basket with a duck, fruit, onions, spices, curry paste, potatoes, tomatoes.

"You say to*may*toes and I say to*mah*toes!" he sang giddily.

Later they sat at one of those round marble-topped tables in a corner Chinese coffee shop, drinking Coke and smoking cigarettes and Milly recalled when she was in school and all the students would gather before class in a shop like this to drink coffee and eat pastries. And soon, prodded by Jim's silent attention, she was remembering aloud her school days. She told her story without a trace of self pity for the sad parts but with a happy enthusiasm for a life so far removed from her present one that the simple recollection of it gave her nothing but pleasure.

Her name in those days was Moses, though Jim was not to learn this till days later when she allowed him a fleeting glimpse of her identity card – that cursed piece of laminated paper that prevented her from getting a job, going to school, travelling outside of Singapore, that condemned her to the cramped narrow borders of Bugis Street to earn her living by the exhibition and sale of that very body as a woman's what the card insisted was a man's – and which card holding absolute authority over her life could only be altered by the same surgery to leave her not only physically liberated but legally too, as a legal woman with the right to those other pieces of paper – diploma and marriage licence and passport – that would admit her at last into the life of a normal human being.

This bright May morning with the sunlight flooding in through the open doors of the coffee shop, he leaning on his elbows on the marble-topped table, listening to her story, gazing intently into her animated face, noticing the utterly feminine way her fingers fluttered as they smoked a cigarette, fiddled with a straw, gestured to illustrate her story, and he wondered how in her former life had she ever managed to masquerade as a boy.

Her mother and father came to Singapore from a small Tamil village in southern India. Milly and Jackie were born some years after their older brothers and sisters and were raised together. Milly remembered little of her father, except he was a huge man with a great moustache. He died when she was very young. So fatherless Milly and Jackie were raised in a household of women. They were not allowed to play in the street and when her mother was away they were locked together in her bedroom. Milly grew up adept at woman's tasks, going to market with her mother, cooking, washing, cleaning, sewing.

The family was Catholic and Milly attended Catholic school as had Jim and like Catholics the world over they had common memories to compare. She told him of school pageants and religious processions, of making flower arrangements and shrines to the Blessed Virgin in the month of May, the prayers they recited and the hymns they sang.

She told him of life in her village, the Indian and Malay and Chinese festivals that marked their lives, of the way people celebrated weddings and mourned their dead.

All this was before her adolescence, her painful lonely years in Catholic high school when she knew herself to be "different" and easy prey for ridicule, the cheap sadism of schoolboys.

"Did you finish high school?" he asked her.

"No, I failed my Cambridge exams. I had so many problems, I was so confused at the time I couldn't concentrate. My life then was such a hell."

"Were you a good student?"

"I was in the subjects I liked. I was no good in math."

"Me neither. Would you want to go back to school? I mean, had you been born the way should have you'd be graduating college right now. Do you ever think of trying to pass the Cambridge exams, going to college?"

It pained him to see how criminally her intelligence had been wasted. She was smart, sensitive, alert, open. She was funny, quick-witted, beat him regularly at Scrabble. There was all this wonderful potential in her yet over the past four years she'd been letting her mind wither, evaporate on frivolities, wrapped up and utterly absorbed in her own sexuality. It saddened him to think of the waste of all her talents. He hoped that someday she could get serious about her life. He feared that what nebulous plans she had for her future were wrapped in some low women's magazine fantasy of jewels and champagne and chic restaurants, the life of an elegant courtesan on the Riviera. Perhaps behind her lack of real future ambitions was the unspoken assumption that she need do nothing but remain beautiful and there would always be men to support her.

But these thoughts would come very much later to him. That May morning as he listened to her tell of her past he could see only endless possibility to her future. Ever the man, the American, he was already making plans for her.

She told him that the persecution she endured at the hands of her classmates grew so harsh, so merciless, so oppressive that she finally screwed up the courage to speak to the headmaster, telling him frankly what her problem was and asking for his help. The priest would prove to be one of her few allies, an understanding protector.

Her sole consolation during this time was working with children in a church group, organizing them for games and outings and art projects. While the whole world turned menacingly against her, when the constant jeering and harassment became unbearable, she could relax and be herself with children.

"I love children," she said. "Because children don't demand anything of your except that you like them and be with them."

She remembered an oratorical contest at school when she had to stand before the whole assembly of students and deliver a speech and the moment she began to speak, with the first words barely out of her mouth, the whole auditorium erupted into howling laughter.

And though her manner of telling her tale was not at all a plea for pity, told in a detached nostalgic tone of voice, Jim could not help but feel a warm out-rushing flow of sympathy for her and inwardly a sharp stab of guilty shame. For there had been boys like Moses in his school too, and Jim's mocking laugh had been among the loudest.

- 15 -

He carried the basket of provisions back to Milly's house and promised to be back for lunch as soon as possible and raced off to his boat to work in a happy singing frenzy sanding down woodwork and then grimy, in dirty shorts, sweaty with wood dust still sticking to arms and face, he hailed a cab and sped back to Milly's house just in time to meet Jackie and her French boyfriend Marcel coming out the door.

"I'm sorry I'm late. I had to finish my work."

"I waited for you," Milly said.

"Yeah, I know but I had to finish the job. What could I do?"

He took a hot shower. She came to the door to hand him a towel.

"I waited for you," she said.

"Aw, come on, baby. I'm *sorry*. I really am. But I can't leave Erik to do all the work."

Downstairs, she served him a delicious duck curry and he ate with enormous appetite, happy in her loving care of him, content to be her man.

Later, waiting for the Changi bus, he told her he was really twenty-eight.

"You *lied* to me!" she cried.

"Yeah, well, shit, you know."

"Jim, you lied to me. Why did you lie to me?"

No excuse would suffice. Her passion for honesty was absolute.

Their heads close together on the crowded bus, talking loudly over the motor's roar, they continued reminiscing about their days in Catholic school.

"I had Dominicans," he said. "What kind of nuns taught you?"

She smiled, putting her lips to his ear to tell him, "We didn't have nuns. I went to a boy's school, remember?"

"Oh yeah," he laughed. "I keep forgetting."

Out on the beach he raced her down the sand to dive yelling into the sea. Later they strolled down the beach still wet, letting the sun dry them. He marveled at how her wet mahogany skin glistened in the sun, the way her long hair hung limp and lank about her shoulders. He asked her then that when she had gotten rid of Derek and undergone and recovered from her operation, if she would consider coming to Africa. He told her he was serious about her and believed they could have a future together.

"Jim, you don't know me."

"That's right. But I'd like to."

– 16–

But he did not even know himself, what hidden conflicts were moiling and seething within him.

That night he was mounted on top of her and driving deeper and deeper up into her and she with her arms and legs tight around him, bucking and writhing beneath him, and as they both rose in rhythm and giddy ecstasy toward some grand commingling of their souls, the sudden and perverse realization entered into his mind that he was fucking a boy.

And instantly his lovemaking turned to fucking with hatred and violence and when he came in a blind spasm of self-loathing, an inner voice was screaming: My God, what's happening to me?

The burden of illusion was too heavy to bear, laying between her legs, feeling her still swollen and stiff beneath the soggy towel. Hiding his horror, he kissed her.

When Milly left the room to shower, Jim stumbled weakly into the bathroom and stared at himself in the mirror over the sink, undergoing a long chilling moment of terror as he looked at his face and his face said to him: I have just had my brains fucked out by a twenty-one-year-old boy.

Badly shaken, he sat down on the toilet bowl and put his head in his hands. What was he getting into?

Slowly he steadied himself, banishing from his mind a sudden ugly image of her as a depraved boy. Nothing could alter the fact that she was, after all, Milly. It was not her fault. He had to believe in her, cast away all doubt. Believe in her as she believed in herself. It was all crazy but he loved her. No matter what would happen he would try to stay with her, try to understand. For was she not the woman fated for him?

- 17 -

Understanding her would not come easy. The next day she received a telegram from Derek in Penang saying his money had been stolen and for her to empty their joint bank account. The entire day she was worried, sullen, withdrawn, depressed. Jim did not help matters by insisting on making love to her. Touched by her sadness, he tried to arouse her, to give her what comfort and oblivion his body would offer, and at the crucial moment of penetration he went limp.

"Oh Jim! Jim!" she wailed as if he had slapped her. At the very moment of taking her, he had lost his nerve, his belief in her, and in the sharp miserable edge to her voice as she called his name he read searing pain, bitter rejection, black despair. She shoved him away and rolled over on her side away from him.

She lay in silence, still as a wounded animal, and Jim laid his cheek against her bare back murmuring, "I'm sorry, Milly. I'm so sorry," a craven plea for absolution for his mortal sin of doubt, the words meaningless before the enormity of her hurt and the howling fury of his own self-loathing.

In time she moved off the bed and went downstairs to sit on the sofa smoking cigarette after cigarette, alone in her misery. When Jim joined her, she did not want to talk to him, despised his phony speeches and only wanted him out of her house, and he, though tempted to say "I'll leave you alone," knew this was no way out for one hoping to be her lover and doggedly he slogged his way through her insults, her accusations that he felt nothing for her, that to him she was just a freak experience, that he was simply using her as material for his book, and he endured her long agonizing silences, pleaded with her to trust him, trying desperately to get her to talk of all that was troubling her, even once singing a bitter Dylan song – "I can't understand, she let go of my hand ..." – to show his own bitterness at her cruel silence.

A long weary hideous night lay in store for them, leaving them both spent, drained, exhausted. It ended with Jim chastened and battered, struggling to keep awake and attentive at five in the morning as Milly finally completed the unfolding of her history.

She told him of her first schoolboy love and the group of five young queens with whom she banded together in defence against the world, of the old queen who taught her about makeup and dress, of the continual inner battle that raged in her, her desire to keep the love and understanding of her family and her crying need to be herself, how at home she did the cooking and washing and struggled to keep the house neat and clean (for even then she must have suffered the foreboding intuition that she would inevitably be forced to abandon it), how she lived surrounded by the malicious gossip of neighbors, the taunts of schoolboys, the censure of teachers and priests – her own religious training denied her the right to existence – and against all these mighty forces stood only her female soul, her implacable, indomitable, relentless determination to be a woman, and so in the end only her own fierce sense of self, her own unswerving will to be who she was, her own steadfast unconquerable courage would liberate her from the chains of false identity society sought to impose on her. Moses died, and Milly was born.

She would be Milly and, unflinching, she would pay the price, the repudiation of her mother and family, exile from home and village, and at age seventeen she entered into the only sanctuary in Singapore where Milly could live and her soul be saved: Bugis Street.

She would never look back, never regret her decision to seize her own personality, and forevermore would refuse any compromise with her own sexuality, abandoning forever male clothing and male ways, and when summoned for military service she boldly appeared in a dress and makeup as the person she really was: Milly.

Jackie had paved the way for her. Jackie had done her stint in the army ("A joke," Milly said. "Working in a storeroom on Sentosa and giving blowjobs behind the stacks."), and then made her debut on Bugis Street. And now Bugis Street took Milly in. It was there but two weeks after her arrival that the village girl met the English second mate.

Four years later, she lay in bed with the beer-bellied American and told him how her first happy years with the Englishman had eventually degenerated into an ugly sordid dreary existence of temper tantrums and beatings.

She talked and talked and talked, and he listened intently, fighting off his weariness, sharing her sorrow yet glad to at last be coming to know her, grateful for the gift she was giving him, trying to understand.

She talked a great deal about Derek. With her shrewd grasp of character, she analysed him with cold brilliant insight, rambling on and on till Jim was sick of hearing about him. It made him uneasy to hear her talk so knowingly about his rival, for rival he considered Derek to be, not fully trusting in Milly's declaration: "I feel nothing for him. I don't love him anymore and I don't hate him. I just want him to leave me alone, leave me in peace," not knowing how truly she spoke, little realizing then how ephemeral her love could be, how shallow the wellsprings of her feelings, and how easily evaporated.

Finally, they slept. They had come to an understanding that night, and made some hard-won progress in the approximation of their two separate souls.

– 18 –

The next day Erik and Jim and Milly were up in a cable car high over the green waters of Singapore's south channel heading for the island of Sentosa, laughing, smoking dope, jabbering as excitedly as three school kids on holiday. Milly showed them where a Japanese bomb crater was still visible as the gardens and terraces of Sentosa loomed closer.

They rented bicycles and explored the steep winding hill trails of the island. They rode their bikes through old wartime cantonments and later in an abandoned playground they smoked more dope and cavorted like children on the rusty swings and slides. Finally they pedalled down to the beach, gliding down a long sweeping hill to the sea. Resplendent in a bright blue scarf and white Indian blouse, Milly was pedalling merrily on her bike, her brown face gleaming with sweat, grinning – and Jim, riding alongside her, then believing he would never see Singapore again and not yet daring to hope that she would really join him in Africa, thought that this was the best he could do for her: to give her times like this, carefree and laughing. It is enough if I can open her heart to see that God's creation is big and beautiful, enough that she share for these weeks my old wild lust for freedom.

This would be his best and only gift to her.

– 19 –

The gift was destined to be delayed for some days.

They had eaten supper and Milly was washing the dishes in the kitchen while Jim sat in an easy chair reading the paper. There came a creaking sound as the gate outside swung open, then a key fitted into the door and the door swung open only to halted by a short length of chain and a white hand reached in frantically trying to undo it and then with the explosive sound of a gunshot the door was kicked open and a red-faced Englishman came stalking inside, Derek raging mad. And Jim still sat with a matchstick in his mouth, legs crossed, newspaper in front of him, not alarmed or frightened or feeling anything but simply infinitely slow in reacting.

"Who are you? Derek demanded angrily.

"Jim," he replied, his head turned, newspaper still held before him.

"Well, get the hell out. This is my house."

Jim nodded his head several times, put the newspaper aside carefully, rose slowly from the chair. "Okay," he said. "It's your house."

"And take off my bloody clothes."

Jim stared at him for a long moment, then realized he meant the sarong he was wearing. "Sure," he said.

Ambling into the kitchen, he saw Milly standing bolt upright and wide-eyed against the sink. "I guess I'd better go, baby," he told her and went into the laundry room where, pulling on his jeans, he heard Derek yelling, "Is that what you've been fucking? *That?* A bloody American? Oh, you must have been really desperate."

Jim in the next room heard all this but reacted to none of it, his thinking processes dulled and slow, wondering what he should do, knew instinctively by the age old masculine rules of the situation that having violated the other man's home and mistress of four years, he had no right to fight back unless sorely provoked, and otherwise was bound to leave house and woman to their returning owner and keeper, and yet another part of him both feared and yearned for such provocation. Feared because he had never had a real fight in his life, and yearned because it was going to be damned difficult to leave this house with any dignity and fighting the bastard would make everything so simple.

So he left his clothes behind in the duffel bag in mute testimony of his intention to return and, taking a deep breath, he stepped into the kitchen. He looked at Derek, waiting for the provocation – the curse, the swung punch, or maybe a shameless attack on Milly – but Derek seemed content to pace about fuming, and Jim went into the living room with Derek following behind him saying, "Go on upstairs and get your things. No, I'll go up and get them, you stay here."

"Don't bother," Jim said. "There aren't any things."

They stood face to face now in the living room, Derek red-faced and wild-eyed and Jim strangely calm, still chewing slowly on the matchstick.

"How much are you paying her?" Derek demanded. "Well, you're going to give her more money."

This is it, Jim thought. The provocation. His heart was beating wildly now, the adrenaline pumping, nerves and muscles coiled and tense, ready to spring, to meet the inevitable onslaught. He stayed silent, glaring steadily into Derek's face.

Then the moment was over. There would be no fight.

Jim picked up his guitar.

"Serenading her, were you?"

"That's right."

"Well, get out," Derek said, racing to the door and flinging it open.

And Jim, still languidly chewing on the matchstick, still holding his gaze on Derek's face, sauntered slowly to the doorway, passed through it, and the door slammed behind him.

When he got to the gate and found it was locked, he could not resist one last face-saving gesture of easy defiance. He returned to the door, rang the bell. The door was flung open and Derek stood glaring at him.

"Ah, the gate's locked," Jim said. "Mind opening it?"

For a long moment, Derek stood speechless, bug-eyed, mouth working in an apoplexy of rage, till he finally blurted out, "Climb over it then. You crawled *under* it to get in here, you can bloody well climb *over* it to get out."

Then he slammed the door in his face.

Heartsick, Jim had to admit this was a good last line. He slunk down the street feeling like a whipped dog. There was no pride to be salvaged: the unalterable fact was Derek was in the house with Milly and Jim was out on the street with his guitar. Then he heard the sound of dishes crashing, Derek yelling. He stopped and waited forlorn in the street, waiting for Milly's scream, her calls for his help. But he knew there would be none, and there weren't.

– 20 –

Back at the Oasis, he telephoned Jackie, told her what had happened, asked her to go out to Changi to make sure that Milly was all right.

"I don't know if I should go out there again," he said.

"No, stay out of it. It is the end of their romance. He is going back to England and she will be free of him. It is best to forget about Milly. If you want another girl, I can find one for you and—"

"No! Goddammit no, I don't want any girl. Just go out there for me tomorrow. I'll call you tomorrow."

Next day, he was drinking beer with Erik and an Australian at Raffles Hotel when he slipped away to telephone. Jackie told him that Milly was all right but that Derek had found his clothes and burned them. Jim thought of his best shirt, a forty-dollar Flamingo football jersey from Brazil, burned. And suddenly elated, he knew he now had the provocation to fight Derek. He was going out to Changi that night.

When the Australian left, Jim told Erik what had happened and what he planned to do.

"Goddamn, I had two good pairs of jeans in that bag," Erik said. "Let's go beat the shit out of that English bastard."

"Well, you can come with me, stay outside the house

in case you hear a gunshot or anything. But it's my fault and my responsibility. So I do all the talking, and I do all the fighting."

It was a black rainy night on the other side of the window of the Changi bus and Jim asked his reflection, "How do you get yourself into these things?"

For the first time in his adult life he was deliberately setting out to fight another human being and absurdly over a pile of dirty laundry serving as the flimsy pretext for the true test, the true confrontation with the most morally serious issue of his life: did he love Milly? He was fighting for Milly, not to show he was brave or handy with his fists – whether he beat the Englishman senseless or was beaten senseless by the Englishman ultimately did not matter much – but he owed it to himself, to the sense of his own integrity and the seriousness of his intentions toward Milly. The provocation had been given and the situation demanded that he undergo the primitive male ritual of fistfighting in order to restore his self respect, that he prove worthy to love and be loved.

Knowing all this but not bothering to articulate it, knowing simply the necessity to do what he was going to do, he stood in the rain before 5 Jalan Meragi and rang the bell, heart thumping wildly, clenching his fists, waiting only for Derek to open the door to speak the necessary justification – "Where the fuck are my clothes?" – before swinging the first punch.

But it was Milly who opened the door. Derek had packed up and moved to a hotel.

- 21 -

They stayed for several hours. Milly showed them the scrapes on her arms, the damage Derek had done to her living room. Milly and Jim sat together on the sofa and talked and talked. Erik drank most of a bottle of Scotch but Jim stayed sober, wary of Derek's return, still ready to fight. Erik got drunk, staggering around the room, yelling, "So where the fuck is he? What hotel is he staying at?"

"Let it be, buddy," Jim said.

She told him she would see him in a couple days. Any day at noon he would be on the boat, he promised her.

The rest of the night Erik and Jim played out the farcical comedy of two friends, one wildly drunk and the other sober and trying to restrain him. On the bus back to town Erik suddenly yelled, "Cukky? Choopy?"

"What? What are you saying?"

"That word Milly told you, choppy? Cucky?"

Oh Christ, Jim thought, here we are on a bus full of Chinese and he's trying to yell out "chokey" – the nigger word for Chinese. Jim began talking rapidly in African Krio to distract him and for the rest of the hour ride they shouted and argued in Krio before an audience of silent, baffled, amused passengers.

They wound up in the Katong Amusement Park, Erik staggering about and yelling, slamming pinball machines about, talking volubly to total strangers. They finished the night in a bar with Erik in an incoherent but passionate argument about Communism with the bartender and Jim talking about sailing with two Chinese businessmen and through it all he felt wonderful, restored to himself, his mind's eye ever fixed on the happy fact that Milly was coming to see him again.

– 22 –

Sunday Erik and Jim went to church at St. Andrew's Cathedral in thanksgiving for having made it from Manila to Singapore, and he prayed for her, careful not to ask God that she come to love him, nor that she meet him in Africa, nor that she even show up at the boat soon, but he simply prayed for her, telling God she had suffered enough, to let her attain the womanhood He had denied her at birth, that she have the chance to realize her great potential, that she find freedom and happiness.

And that night he lay on the cabin roof of the boat reading by lantern light the novel she had lent him,

Sayonara, the story of the love of an American man and an Asian woman over twenty years ago. And when he finished the book he sat looking up at the stars and reflected that all his pent-up passions were at last released and running rampant and there was no room and no time for reflection. He was exhilarated by the unbridled sprawl of his liberated emotions. He was living intensely day by day, and he would commit none of it to paper. He abandoned his twelve thousand-word project, made no daily notes in his journal. He was no longer obsessed with recording the past when his present was so vivid and colorful and giddy and harrowing and charged with meaning. The present, his feelings, his very soul had been restored to him by the miraculous intervention of this Singapore girl. Somewhere in the back of his mind lurked the fearful foreboding that she would ultimately hurt him, cause him to suffer as he had not permitted himself to suffer since his first love had dumped him so many years before. But even this did not matter. For he was alive again, feeling more fully and intensely alive that he had ever dreamed possible. He, a sworn twenty-eight-year-old bachelor, was in love. The world traveler, boozehound, whoremonger, dope smoker, guitar player, samba dancer, ex-seminarian, bullshit artist, con man, amateur agronomist, aspirant writer, blue water sailor – he was in love.

– 23 –

Shortly after noon the next day as he was painting varnish on the cabin doors, he heard her voice call out his name, and saw her standing before the old whitewashed harbor wall – the small dark lithe Indian girl, a big white smile illuminating her brown face, waving to him, a vision of loveliness that would be repeated so many times in the weeks to come, always signalling for him the cessation of ordinary time and routine events, and heralding his entrance into the deep significance, bright clarity, boundless meaning of their sacred time together, a joyous advent into the eternal present of her endlessly unfolding being.

He jumped into the dinghy and rowed to shore as quickly as his arms could pull the oars.

When she was safely settled in the stern, she leaned forward and planted her lips on his and he hungrily devoured her in a long languid delicious kiss. Finally their lips parted and grinning steadily they looked into each other's eyes. He put out his hands and pressed them to the warmth of her cheeks. It's good to see you," he said.

"It's good to see *you*," she replied.

Part Two

They would be together for three more weeks and he would come to love her more, and to believe she loved him.

"You're the only person I can talk to anymore," she told him on one of those bright afternoons when they strolled hand-in-hand away from the Oasis Club and out into the sunshine of the parking lot, out on to the road and the freedom of another day together.

- 2 -

He did not teach her how to swim. Like in so many other things he was merely her appreciative audience, ready to lend support only if she needed it. Those first few times he would swim out to sea a little, doing a strenuous sidestroke with her hanging on to his shoulders and kicking in accompaniment, swimming until she felt it was far enough – further and further from shore each time they went out

– and then he would turn and point them toward shore and she would cast off from him and swim on her own in a determined thrashing freestyle, overcoming her fear of the water in her intent rhythmical surging toward the beach, and he would swim alongside her glorying in her independence. She never needed his help, never failed to reach the shore unaided.

– 3 –

He was not devoid of vanity and her carping on his big belly rankled him, her taunts of "Fat sloppy Yank". "Fat-tay" as her Singaporean accent had it. He was not above worrying about getting old and his beer belly was that of a middle-aged man, an obscene hairy obstacle before her slim youthfulness. He sensed she could only love the handsomest of men just as he was not interested in homely women no matter how splendid their personalities.

He worried about his receding hairline too though she did not mock him for this. "Balding men are highly sexed," she informed him. "I read it in a magazine." And while he thought this was stupid, still, absurdly, it gave him some consolation.

Though she nagged and joked about his fat belly, she did nothing but augment it, for she was a superb cook and prepared amazing feasts for him and took him to her favorite restaurants – Indian places on Serangoon Road where they ate with their fingers off banana leaves, Malay satay shacks on Changi Beach, noisy crowded open-air Chinese curry crab joints on Beach Road – to make sure that he ate like a king. She introduced him to a vast cornucopia of exotic food, a splendid gourmet's delight of oriental dishes, and with spoon or fork or chopsticks or his own eager fingers, Jim would greedily devour heaping portions of everything in sight, closing his eyes in rapture to savor yet another new discovery in taste, moaning with pleasure, grunting, grinning.

"I love to watch you eat," she said, making him laugh. "No, Jim, really. You seem to take so much pleasure in everything you eat."

And he grunting with his mouth full, "That's because everything's so goddamn good."

In the night market across the street from Cold Storage, she would flit from stall to stall ordering in Tamil or Hokkien or Malay a whole table full of savory dishes, spicy mutton, sweet succulent prawns, exquisite combinations of vegetables and fish. And afterward they would sit sipping tea and watch the busy concourse of people passing, loving couples and young families, running children and doddering grandfolks, Malay and European and Indian and Chinese, the whole spectrum gaudy and multi-colored of the great melting pot of Singapore.

"You know," he said, "I really like this town."

- 4 -

They went to an art exhibit in the library off the park. She showed a strange lack of interest in the paintings till he had the sudden inspiration to lend her his glasses.

"Are the pictures clearer now?" he asked her.

"Yes!" she cried, her face beaming with pleasure.

"You mean you see things better with my glasses on?"

"Oh yes. Look at this painting here. See the mother's face, how sorrowful she looks?"

"Baby, if you see things better with Jim's glasses on, you really need glasses. When did you last have your eyes checked?"

"Oh I know I need glasses. I just haven't got around to it."

"Sure. It's just that you're vain. Vanity, thy name is woman."

Later in the big corner bookstore by the park, they lingered in the art books section, leaning on each other as they browsed through books Jim picked out of his favorite artists. The picture Milly liked best was Andrew Wyeth's "Johanna's World", that tiny mysterious woman laying in the dry grass field and looking up at the stark barn on the hill. As they walked down the street afterward, he told her excitedly about New York and its art galleries and big museums and she laughed and said, "You're always saying how much you hate New York and how you'll never go back there but you really miss it. In your heart you really do love it. You're so proud of being from New York."

"New York is like an old girlfriend, Milly. I love her and I hate her."

— 5—

One day they sat close together in the cabin of the boat, passing a joint back and forth as he showed her his photographs, each picture a window on his past. But the window that most held her attention was the small round one that reflected back her own face: the compact mirror she was never without. She propped it up on the galley table and began the slow meticulous preparation of her face to venture out into the world, the methodical infinitely painstaking ministration with brush and lipstick and eyebrow pencil. She arranged and rearranged her hair, played around with her bright blue scarf, striking poses before the mirror, and Jim a willing participant in her narcissism, the ever-fascinated spectator to her show, suggested that now she looked like a Brazilian girl from Bahia, and now an African girlfriend, and now a beautiful Polynesian girl from the South Seas needing only an orchid behind her ear. Clowning around, laughing, she snatched off his glasses and put them on. "Ah," he said. "Now you're a college girl." And when she pulled off her scarf and pulled her hair back into a severe bun, he said, "And now you're a schoolteacher."

"Class, take out your pencils and books," she snapped, gazing happily in rapt contemplation at her mirrored face, and smiling her secret smile.

– 6 –

There would come a time, a bitter angry time, when Jim would conclude that Milly was really in love with her mirror self. And that the roots to her pernicious and self-destructive narcissism lay buried deep in her childhood and painful adolescence when the whole great powerful terrifying world was demanding that she be a boy and only the mirror told her differently. Only in the mirror did she receive the assurance that yes she was a woman, and a beautiful woman. And that her true self is locked somewhere inside that mirror, enslaved to it, and afraid to come out, to be a real living breathing woman in the real world, to grapple and grow with a real man. And that Jim abetted in her narcissism, encouraged her with his uncritical wide-eyed adulation, his enthusiastic audience of one only enhanced the illusion for her. But Jim was not needed to maintain the illusion. The mirror was enough.

- 7 -

If Milly's vice was mirrors, Jim was helplessly addicted to bookstores. He had searched out bookstores in scores of cities to find hours of peace in their quiet sanctuary. It seemed to him that bookstores whether in Rio or Dublin or New York or Lagos or Manila were really but one big bookstore – a magical universe far removed from the ordinary routine world where great stories were his for the asking, where long dead persons came to life, and far off places brought close to hand. He loved to prowl down the brightly lit aisles lined with shelf upon shelf of multi-colored book covers, his eyes lingering slowly along each shelf, scutinizing each title, picking books out at random to dip into them, browsing contentedly for hours.

And perhaps his passion for writing was a form of narcissism but little removed from Milly's mirror, for almost everything he wrote was autobiographical and the character based on himself was always the hero on center stage. His writing, at its worst, was self-conscious and self-centered. He was the star of his own drama with all other characters relegated to the periphery. He was continually holding up a literary mirror to himself. What right had he to condemn Milly's preoccupation with her mirror? Her narcissism was but a simpler and more direct form of his own.

- 8 -

They were in a bookstore – Jim, Milly and Erik – above Cold Storage. And Jim, though short of cash now, could not resist buying a handful of books. They ate a leisurely lunch at the Salad Bowl restaurant, skimming through *Time* and *Newsweek* and *Cosmopolitan*, reading things aloud, making joking comments, fooling around. Milly left to change into her shorts and then met them on the sidewalk wearing her new blue sneakers.

Leaving Erik, Jim and Milly took a cab to Changi and met her best friend Sarah and her boyfriend Bill on the beach. The four of them frolicked in the water, the boys putting the girls up on their shoulders to play chickenfights, and then rested, lolling in the shallow water. Up on the beach, Milly and Sarah got into a mock fight on top of an overturned rowboat which lurched to the side suddenly, spilling them, screaming, into the sand.

Then Jim and Milly headed off down the beach for a thatch-roofed Malay restaurant.

They sat facing each other, holding hands, their faces

close together, talking rapidly and then lapsing into happy silence, staring intently into each other's eyes, bound together in an almost unbearable mystic unity, each lost in rapt contemplation of the other.

The delicate way she dipped her head to spoon up lichees send a sudden warm spasm of joy coursing through him and with the sea and the setting sun behind her he knew he had never seen her so beautiful. The moment was sacred and he wished it would never end. It never would, in his memory.

Stumblingly, haltingly, he tried to tell her of his feelings but failed, ending up lamely saying, "I'll always remember this moment, Milly."

"You'll always remember this moment till you meet the next girl."

He shook his head, knowing there would be no next girl. He could not trust himself to speak but simply leaned forward in mute supplication for the blessing of her lips.

– 9 –

He cooked steak and spaghetti one night on the boat and he and Erik and Milly ate by lantern light on the white roof of the cabin. Milly cleared away the dishes then and went down below to make coffee.

"There's something to be said for Asian women," Erik said.

"She's a good girl," Jim said.

"She sure treats you right, buddy. You got a good deal going. I like her."

They drank coffee, smoked dope, listened to Dylan's "Blood on the Tracks", enjoyed the serenity of the night.

A white dinghy appeared out of the night, sculled by a thin blond kid, English, who Erik introduced as John from the yacht beside them. An ex-British explosives expert with a year in Belfast under his belt, John was sailing around the world with his parents.

Erik and John drank Scotch in the cockpit while Jim and Milly stretched out on two mattresses, a Scrabble game between them, kidding each other in mock rivalry. She beat him, as usual, then they went out on the bowsprit to be alone.

A quiet night on the waters, the splendor of the stars, the lights of the tall buildings along the shoreline thrust up into the black bowl of the night and the line of yellow lamp-lights along Katong Bridge reflected in the black waters of the canal, and the great grey circular bulk of the National Stadium illuminated by a thousand spotlights and nearby the festive lights – red, green, blue, white, yellow – festooned along the circular roof of the Oasis Club, the colors glimmering and sparkling and shimmering on the black waters, a constantly changing mosaic, like living stained glass, and she out on the bowsprit, her bare feet planted along the wooden beam and her arms held over her head to grip the thick cable of the forestay, and he standing close behind her, his arms around her, her plump bottom snug up against him.

"I like being like this," she said. "Over the water like I am and any moment I could fall. I'm a courageous girl."

"You are, Milly. And you should feel what it's like when the boat is sailing and all the sails are billowed out with the wind and the whole boat is tipped over and gliding through the water and then it's the most wonderful feeling to stand out here as the boat rises and falls and dips down and lifts up again," he said, dipping and swaying his body in imitation of the sea's motion and his arms around her pulling her gently from side to side and giggling she snuggled down into his arms, saying, "I'd like that. I like being a tomboy. I like doing the things we've been doing. Jim, you're so good to me. What are you so good to me?"

"You're good to me, Milly. You've been so kind."

- 10 -

He loved to watch her smoke dope. That night in the lantern light of the cabin, her hands dark against the shiny wood of the table, shredding the buddha sticks and mixing the grass with tobacco, how nimbly her deft slender fingers rolled a joint, the precise way her long pink nails handled a roach. She could manage a feeble gasping dying ember and still pass more to give Jim.

And he loved to watch the pleasure seeping into the contours of her face, the dreamy look in her great black eyes, and with the vision of her timeless joy before him he would enter with her into that slow languorous gentle rhythm – a void of tranquil bliss.

- 11 -

Then he was into her, slowly churning around inside her, and then he began to ride her, slowly at first and then spurring her on faster and faster, then slowing again, teasing her, pulling himself nearly out of her only to thrust back into her to the hilt, and then riding her in earnest now and she suddenly into his rhythm, moaning and squirming and wiggling under him, arms tight around him, bucking furiously, meeting his every thrust with equal force, taking faster and faster the blows of his ravenous entry, faster and harder and stronger and more urgent they galloped together in a single conjoined desperate rhythm till he felt her stiffen, rise under him, and she cried out, wailing in a long exultation of abandoned joy, shuddering helplessly under him and he let himself go, felt himself surge outward, flaming, out of his body and his flash and fire and soul gone gone gone into her, both mingled now in a cosmic meeting point beyond bodies where womansoul and mansoul touch.

They lay still, silent, spent, the deep slumberous peace finally broken by her question, "Do you like making love to me?"

And he stretched out on top of her, feeling like an exhausted angel, a dying god, a mythic hero come back from the farthest of cosmic journeys, could only murmur, "Yes. Yes baby. Oh yes."

- 12 -

"I didn't like that Englishman last night," she said as she sipped her morning tea on the boat's deck. "I didn't like the way she was looking at me while we were playing Monopoly. He kept giving me strange looks and shaking his head."

"Well, you know, the Pommies are a strange race."

Some nights later, Jim and Erik and John the Englishman were drinking beer at a bar in the amusement park. They were on their third or fourth beer when the Englishman said, "Let me ask you something, Jim. You won't get angry, will you?"

"What?"

"Promise not to get angry now. But what I want to know is, your girlfriend Milly, is she really a girl?"

"What? *What*? What the *fuck* kind of question is that?"

"Now don't get angry now."

Jim turned to Erik saying, "Did I hear that fuckhead ask me if Milly was a girl?"

"I was only asking. Don't be angry."

"Who is this asshole?" he demanded of Erik.

"Aw come on, buddy," Erik said. "He just wants to know if Milly's got a cunt. She's got a cunt, doesn't she?"

"Yeah she's got a cunt."

"I'm sorry," John said. "It's just that having been down to Bugis Street the night before made me suspicious. I mean that deep voice she has and the phony eyebrows—"

"Look, I don't want to hear another word from you about Milly. You understand?"

"Quite," John said, looking down into his beer.

"Come on, you guys, drink up," Erik said.

Jim left the bar early to be on the boat at ten when Milly said would show up if she could. When Erik came home later that night, he found Jim asleep on the cabin roof in the light of the electric lantern.

"I'm worried about you, buddy," Erik said the next morning. "Leaving the bar early, sleeping topside waiting for Milly. You seem like you're really serious about this girl. You're not in love or anything like that, are you?"

But Jim could no more admit that than admit the secret his lover laboured under.

- 13 -

They would pass hour after hour in conversation, telling each other the smallest details of things that had happened in the hours they had been separated, recalling a thousand tiny incidents from their past lives, telling of their dreams and likes and dislikes and worries and ambitions, and there were times when he felt he was her only friend, and times when he knew she trusted not even him.

"You still don't believe in me, do you?" he'd ask her.

"I can't. Oh Jim, I've had so many men. I can't believe you. Understand me. Please understand me."

- 14 -

They went to Sentosa a second time, bicycling down to the beach and going swimming, and returned the rental bikes an hour late because Milly's watch had stopped, then tired and thirsty drinking tall glasses of iced tea at the snack shop.

Jim was nearly broke now, having telegraphed for money the day before, so they stopped near Clifford Pier so Milly could change some Swedish krona, then they strolled over a bridge spanning the nearby Singapore River.

They sat in the evening breeze at a table on the terrace of an outdoor restaurant overlooking the river and the anchored rows of old green-roofed Chinese barges, each with a painted eye in the prow. They sipped that thick sweet orange Indian tea and talked for an hour, tired, happy, relaxed after the strenuous day, watching the sun set over the jumbled red tile roofs of the old shophouses lining the banks of the river. They left the restaurant and passed the statue of Sir Stanford Raffles and Milly read aloud the inscription at the base, told him something of the early history of Singapore and said, "You know, I'm proud to be a Singaporean. Wherever I go in the world I'll always be proud to tell people I'm from Singapore."

They returned to Changi and she cooked dinner for him and later as they were playing Scrabble she said, "You know I have to go to work tonight."

He looked at her face for a long silent hopeless moment.

"Sure," he said.

"You don't mind, do you?"

"Of course I mind but there's nothing I can do

about it."

Stung, she cried out, "What do you expect? I have to provide for my future."

"I know. I know."

"I mean, no one is ever going to *give* me anything. I've got to look after myself. I can't help what I am."

"And I can't help how I feel."

He sat before the television for an hour while upstairs she got ready to go out. The television was so much meaningless noise and images for he was deafened and blinded by his outraged feelings. He felt helpless and sordid and guilty before the harsh fact that the woman he claimed to love was going out on the street.

In a few weeks he was sailing to Africa. He would not give up his freedom now to take responsibility for her and so forfeited any right to demand anything from her. He had promised to take care of her once she reached him in Africa, and meant that promise with all that was true in him, but Africa was a long way away, and his promises did not pay the rent.

Lonely and bored, he climbed the stairs to be with her and found her sitting in her G-string before her dressing table mirror, a bright spotlight fixed on her. He lay on her bed and watched with a slowly mounting sense of horror as she painted her face into that of an outlandish stranger, an eerie vacant inhuman parody of a woman. The room seemed suddenly charged with the unreal atmosphere of a stage dressing room and with bleary dismay Jim watched his beloved apply lipstick, rouge, powder, false eyelashes to slowly transform herself into the cheap gaudy image of a Bugis Street whore. And Jim was suddenly afraid that of all the roles and poses that Milly used, this outrageous mask of a flamboyant whore came closest to the real.

She claimed to be sick of Bugis Street. "I feel like an animal in a zoo, a strange animal in a cage with everyone looking at me." Yet perhaps she was afraid of the world outside that unreal zoo cage and had come to need her captivity. Maybe she just enjoyed the attention and could not live without it and was deeply afraid of being an ordinary woman and not the queen of the freak show, the star attraction of the zoo.

Yes, he was afraid for her and afraid for himself. His old Catholic morality reasserted itself. There was something sinister in the painstaking devotion with which Milly created the evil image that stared back at her from the mirror. He remembered Milly telling him about old queens who dabbled in black magic and horror-struck, watching Milly transform herself into this monstrous stranger, he wondered if this was not the Devil's work.

Shaken, he left her bedroom and went to wait for her downstairs.

She came down the stairs then in a red silk evening gown, wigged, high-heeled, in that strange painted face.

"How do I look?" she asked him. "If you saw me on

113

Bugis Street, you wouldn't recognize me, would you?"

"No, baby," he said sadly. "I wouldn't."

She dropped him off in her taxi on the way to Bugis Street. He was silent and depressed the whole trip. Then he saw he was making her miserable too, and tried to hide his feelings with jokes. The next night in the same taxi with the same destination, he would sing all through the long dark dreary ride, singing sad songs for her, and for himself.

– 15 –

Days passed and still no money from the States. Milly was more or less supporting Jim and Erik, buying them beers and meals, paying for taxis and movie tickets. She took Jim to the Singapore Museum. They ambled arm-in-arm from exhibit to exhibit – pottery and swords and krises and furniture and jewelled costumes – she telling him the history of sultans and colonists, wars and rebellions, the customs and culture of Malay and Chinese and Indian. Every so often in hidden corners of that great vaulted many-chambered building, they'd clinch in a furtive kiss.

When the museum closed, they went to the restaurant in front of the library to sip Indian tea and smoke cigarettes and watch the people passing on the sidewalk.

Jim noticed a gorgeous Indian girl, huskier than Milly but with the very similar facial features.

"Jim, do you see that girl? That Indian girl in the green dress?"

"Yes."

"I know her. She's from my village."

The girl entered the restaurant with some friends and took a table somewhere behind Jim.

As they continued talking, Jim could see that Milly was ill at ease, uncomfortable, aware of the other girl's scrutiny.

"Jim," she said suddenly. "Kiss me."

And he knew why and was happy to do it.

- 16 -

It was a Saturday that she told him about the Frenchman, an old neighbor and friend she said, who had offered to let her use his apartment when Derek left. "He's out of town a lot on oil rigs so it will be very convenient. I met him yesterday, didn't I? I'm to have lunch with him today to discuss the details. But I'm going to make it clear to him that there is to be no sex involved."

That night Erik and John went to Bugis Street. So they will meet Milly at work, Jim thought. And tomorrow I tell

Erik yes, she's a Bugis Street whore and I love her.

Erik returned at dawn blind drunk and singing "Going Down Again" at the top of his lungs. He woke Jim to tell him of the night's revels, of a drunk English sea captain and his Chinese first mate, of boisterous Australians and singing Maoris, and how he'd talked to Jackie. And Jim, hearing no mention of Milly, was relieved her secret was safe but strangely ashamed at his own silence.

She turned up Monday morning bearing gifts of curry rice and oranges and grapefruits and helped Jim paint the deck stanchions white.

- 17 -

They were eating a late Chinese lunch at the Oasis when Jim called the Holiday Inn and learned his money had arrived. He raced back to the table, doing a silly jig and singing, "We're in the money! We're in the money!" and thereupon ensured a frantic scramble to get to the American Express office before it closed, Jim rowing out to the boat for his passport and Erik and Milly racing for the road to hail a taxi, when the sky opened up and a heavy torrential downpour instantly drenched them all to the skin. They retreated to the boat for refuge, slept, woke to smoke dope and sing to Jim's guitar, but soon it became obvious that the mood of the evening had changed for Milly. She lay in his bunk listless and despondent and when he asked if she wanted to go home, she said yes.

There was a strained silence in the cab on the way to Changi.

"Hey, what's wrong, Milly?"

"Nothing."

"Tell me."

"I just don't feel so good."

But once in her house, sitting cold and withdrawn on the sofa, she complained that he didn't care for her, that he was going to Africa and she would be left alone and what would happen to her?

"I have to go. I have to do this thing. If I don't, I'll regret it for the rest of my life."

"So you're only thinking of yourself."

"I've got to be free. When I reach Africa, I'll send for you."

"Don't say that if you don't mean it."

"I *do*, baby. I really do. I've never been so serious in my life."

"It does me no good now. What's going to happen to me?"

Around and around the argument went. He was leaving for Africa, she was staying for an uncertain future. In bed then, she said to him, "What if you reach Africa and you change your mind about me, find someone else, and I never hear from you again?"

"Then I'd be a real bastard, wouldn't I?"

"What if I come to Africa and you don't want me anymore, and you leave me with no money in a strange country?"

"No, I'm not that sort of person."

"No? What sort of person are you?"

"Milly, don't you know me at all? Don't you believe in me at all?"

"No."

- 18 -

She came out to the boat the next day sick and feverish with a cold caught the day before. They apologized to each other for the night before. Then he took her back to shore and got a taxi for her. She said she would come back when she felt better and they would make another start.

- 19 -

And start again they did. The next night at the Palm Beach restaurant, gleefully stoned and ravenous from a day at

Tiger Balm Gardens and the Jurong Bird Park, they flung themselves into a merry orgy of eating, ripping apart crabs and prawns, chins slick with hot sauce, fingers gooey, grinning madly at each other.

– 20 –

They stepped down from the Changi bus into a street they had not been before, wandered into an antique shop, browsing happily. The owner was friendly and gave Jim a clove-scented Indonesian cigarette. Then they crossed the street to a corner Chinese restaurant to drink tea and eat duck soup. And suddenly it seemed to him that there was a special quality, intensity, clarity to the morning sunshine that invested everything it touched – the bright yellow wood wall of the building opposite, the ivory-colored chopsticks and marble table and shiny chrome and the smooth brown flesh of Milly's face and bare arms – with the freshness of new morning and Jim felt surging through him a powerful sense of certitude that he and Milly would have a new life of endless possibilities.

They ate chicken curry at Jackie's house with her French boyfriend Marcel, his father and his friend, all three merchant seamen from the same ship, none of whom spoke English. Jackie sat with her legs crossed high in a white baby doll negligee. Around the living room lounged a half dozen other queens: Lisa, owner of the house, tiny Jessie, Tina, the tall Eurasian beauty.

Jim carried on a forced silly discussion with the old man in a garbled mixture of Spanish and Portuguese. Milly, laughing, said, "This is like chickens and ducks."

He sat on the sofa and, suddenly playful, Milly climbed up behind him and threw her legs over his shoulders and laughing, grabbing her thighs, he stood up and ran around the room with her shrieking and hitting him on the head to run faster.

"Milly's got a new husband!" Tina cried.

They went to Thieves Market that day and down Arab Street to the Safari Lounge of the Merlin Hotel to sit in a phony zebra skin booth, holding hands and talking quietly for hours.

— 21 —

They came out of the Lido theater and walked hand-in-hand down Orchard Road to a café they often went to. As they walked they sang "We may never love that this again!" – the song from the movie they'd just seen, "The Towering Inferno". At the café they ordered iced tea and Jim watching the crowds passing on the sidewalk, with

Milly at his side, reflected that it had been weeks since he had gotten drunk. Habitually now he ordered iced tea in place of beer. He laughed inwardly, thinking, If any girl can make you stop drinking beer, watch it, Jim, you're in love.

– 22 –

The morning came when he was to see her at her happiest. He was to meet her in the lobby but missed her by a few minutes. He took the elevator up to the seventh floor and found the psychiatrist's office. He entered and saw the door of the consulting room open and a nurse seeing him said, "I think your friend has come, Miss." And through the open door he saw Milly seated before the doctor's desk. He waved at her and smiled what he hoped was a reassuring smile.

The door closed. He sat down to wait. He held a *Reader's Digest* open before him but read not a word, all his thoughts and worries and hopes somewhere behind the closed door.

Finally it opened and a smiling Milly came out. A flurry of formalities at the nurse's desk and then they were out the door, laughing in relief, striding free down the corridor. He threw his arm over her shoulders and she cried, "I did it, didn't I? I've made the first step!"

"It's a brand new life now, Milly."

"Oh it is! It is! I'm so happy!"

She turned to him, her face transfixed with joy, and wrapped her arms around him and kissed him.

Waiting for her letter to be typed – the one that would admit her to the hospital for her operation – they went into a little park and played around in the grass like children. Jim did somersaults and cartwheels and Milly climbed up in a tree.

Jim climbed the tree after her and clenching his fist to form an imaginary microphone, he imitated a television interviewer: "We're speaking now with Mrs Tarzan, the famous queen of the apes. Come you tell us, Mrs Tarzan, how does it feel living in a tree?"

"Quite comfortable, actually. Except when it rains."

"And how does it feel being married to the King of the Apes? I mean, what do you find to talk about?"

"Oh. Bananas."

Later she told him that when she used to live nearby she would often come to this park to smoke dope at night.

"You know," she said, "it's been days now since we've smoked any dope."

"That's true."

"It's been more than a week since we smoked dope. And you know, I don't miss it. I don't need it with you. I used to need to smoke. I would really miss it when I didn't have any because I used to want to get really crazy when I went to work, I wanted to be really crazy when I made love. But with you I don't need it. I just like making love to you."

– 23 –

She said she was exhausted and was going home to sleep. If she woke early enough, she'd meet him at the Oasis at ten that night. He said he'd be there and wait till eleven.

He went out with Erik and John to an Indian restaurant and then to a bar on Arab Street. Then he caught a cab to the Oasis and waited there drinking beer, smoking a cigar.

Once the glass entrance doors opened and he saw a slim Indian girl in a long white dress coming up the walkway toward him and suddenly he was on his feet, his heart beating rapidly, awash in rapture. But the girl was closer now, and he saw she was a stranger.

So he went back to meet Erik and John on Bugis Street. He wanted a last hard look at the zoo.

- 24 -

Milly was wrong. If Bugis Street was a zoo, the white people were the animals. For the first time in his life Jim was ashamed of being a white man. It was it hideous night, tables full of drunk white faces shouting, braying, cursing, singing, arguing, whooping with beery laugher. And every horror he saw pricked his conscience: for it was here that his leaving consigned Milly. He was surrendering her to the paws of those sweating redfaced animals.

Throughout the night Erik and John carried most of the conversation while Jim sat morosely silent, drinking beer after beer. Jackie came to their table and announced that her operation was set for three weeks away. He congratulated her and wished her every happiness.

Hour later when he was seriously drunk he staggered and weaved his way in search of her and found her seated at the same table he'd first seen her an eternity ago. He collapsed into a chair before her saying, "I wanna talk to you." He was drunk but not so drunk that by a supreme effort of the will he was unable to speak coherently.

"You're the only family Milly has. I wanna know how you feel about Milly and me."

Jackie said it was fine with her if he had the means to support her. Jim replied he did and would and returned to his table.

He got horribly drunk, so drunk that when he stumbled over to a table full of singing Maoris and borrowed a guitar to sing a song he could not make his fingers behave to the chord changes. He sang a sloppy slurred fucked up version of "If I had a Hammer". The Maoris hooted and laughed and held their noses. Some time shortly after that, he blacked out.

He woke up at dawn on some side street of Chinese food stalls. John sat next to him drinking beer. Jim checked his pants pockets. There was still some money in there so at least he hadn't been rolled. A painful throbbing headache pounded behind his eyes and everything seemed hazy, foggy. He lifted a trembling hand to his face: his glasses were gone. Not on the table either. Not anywhere.

- 25 -

He spent Sunday hungover and shaken, his nerves shot, feeling foolish and guilty and ashamed, and asking himself questions like: What the hell am I doing with my life?

- 26 -

Monday morning Milly was at the harbor wall, calling his name, grinning and waving. He hurried to pick her up in the dinghy.

"I missed you," she said.

"I missed you, baby. I've been feeling terrible. God, I got so drunk Saturday night."

"Guess who's come back to town?"

"Derek."

"Right."

"Fuck him. Let's go to Sentosa."

They smoked dope on the boat. Jim was unusually silent. He had taken a psychic beating over the weekend and could not summon much enthusiasm to talk. They returned to shore, walked along the harbor wall in single file and when they reached the end, Milly turned abruptly and with a wide-eyed grief-stricken look on her face asked him, "Are you bored with me?"

And knowing no words would serve, he took her face in his hands and parted her lips with a fierce tongue-plunging kiss.

They bicycled to a part of Sentosa they hadn't been before. Laying in the grass on a hill overlooking a golf course and the sea, they passed a joint and silently enjoyed the view.

"When are you leaving, Jim?"

"A few more days. Maybe Thursday."

"I worry about you. It's such a long way and your boat is so small."

"What you could do is light a candle for me in church."

"I'm going to miss you so much. I don't like to think about what my life will be like when you're gone."

"Think about Africa then. Will you meet me there?"

"I will."

– 27 –

They met in church the next day. They knelt together in a pew before a side altar of the Virgin Mary.

Jim felt his whole life come to a pinnacle as he asked God and all that he held holy to sanction his love for Milly, to protect her, to bring them together again.

They turned then and looked at each other, a long solemn sacred moment, and like sealing a vow, they kissed.

Part Three

So Jim was gone and Milly was left to stay. Jim was gone for three weeks when a letter for Milly arrived at her sister's house. It was a thick, many-paged letter sent from Pontianak in western Borneo, handwritten in a barely legible tight slovenly scrawl on the torn out pages of a ledger-sized journal. The letter told of his two week's sea journey, smashing the bowsprit on a fish trap on their first night out of Singapore, getting caught in a huge horrific storm for three days that blew them up toward Vietnam and then spun them around back to Borneo, making repairs now in this little town up a river called Pontianak. He wrote that his love for her was a solid as the boat he sailed. Milly thought it was a wonderful letter and showed it to her friends. They congratulated her on her good luck in men. Two weeks later a telegram arrived saying, "Arrived Jakarta today. Plan to settle here and teach English. My prayers for your speedy and safe recovery. Letter to follow."

And then on August 1 she was alone in Jackie's house when the phone rang.

"Hello."

"Hello. Could I speak to Jackie please?"

"Hello?"

"Hello, Jackie? This is Jim. Jim Eckardt."

"Jim! This is Milly!"

"MILLY! HEEEY BABY, HOW ARE YA?"

He said he was in Changi Airport, asked her for Jackie's address and rang off saying, "Okay, see you soon."

Then she was coming down the stairs, "Jim?", on the landing now and she saw him, in jeans and army shirt, thinner and bearded, coming up the stairs and "Jiiiiim!" she wailed joyfully, "Jim! Jim! Jim!" hurling herself down the stairs to collide into his embrace, flinging her arms around his neck. He held her tightly – "Oh baby, baby!" – turning and carrying her down the steps to set her down on the floor, their lips already searching, meeting and they were kissing then, lips and tongue frantically seeking to say everything in moments when mere words would take eternity.

Up in Jackie's room, she sitting on the floor and he on the edge of the bed, his breathing heavy from the effort of lugging his gear up the stairs, sweaty, guzzling a Coke, looking at her wild-eyed, grinning, laughing too easily.

"Would you like a joint?"

"Later, Milly. Let me calm down."

They talked. Jim's voice sounded in his ears as cracked and hoarse and disused as a hermit's come off the desert after forty years solitude. His mind was still racing in sailboat and jet plane and taxi to reach his beloved and now he was hearing her voice and seeing her face. She was fatter, more beautiful, healthy and sound and cheerful – not laying wasted and in agony in some hospital bed – she was whole.

She told him about the Frenchman and he told her how he decided not to teach English in Jakarta after all and had come to Singapore and what he had come to Singapore for. How in the solitude of the sea he had come to see himself clearly and was resolved now to begin a life with her. And to begin the serious work of his life, writing.

They smoked a joint and then they were on the floor together in a long kiss. Then he was on the bed as putting on the bright batik shirt and sarong of green and silver damask that he'd brought her from Jakarta, she posed for him and for the mirror behind him. Her beauty was radiant, ethereal, compelling.

"Do you want me?"

"Yes, Milly, I want you."

She pulled the batik shirt over her head, baring her small black-nippled breasts and then she loosened the sarong slowly down her hips, her thighs, and down to her feet and she stood naked before him while an insane shrill voice screamed in Jim's mind: *That's a boy*!

Shocked, a bolt of fear running through him, she still standing naked, expectant, before him and he kept his eyes fastened on her lovely face, repeating like a prayer over

130

and over in his mind: Milly, Milly, Milly, Milly.

And then it was all right and he stretched out his hand to her. They lay naked on the bed together. Jim was trembling, feverish, woozy, his skin burning – was it the flu? Calmer now, he ran his hand over her breasts and belly and thighs, kissed and caressed and fondled her, yet he was still too nervous to become aroused. That could come later, he thought. For the moment he was content just to feel and hold her close to himself.

So the mood changed. She was showing him her photographs in an evening gown, taken by the Frenchman, and they decided to go to Changi beach. There was an uncomfortable interview with Lisa about renting a room for two in the house. And then they were kissing in the back of a speeding cab. Jim was still trying to grasp the joyful reality that he was in Singapore with his girlfriend under his arm.

It was unbearably hot in the cab, sweat poured off him in rivulets, and he had a raging thirst.

They ate Chinese food at a table overlooking the sea. Milly ate ravenously but Jim had no appetite, feeling hot and cold flashes. He didn't know if he was stoned or sick but his heart was throbbing far to fast, he couldn't seem to really catch his breath. He felt he was losing his ease with Milly, his conversation sounding tense and forced.

They strolled barefoot down the line of surf of Changi beach, hand in hand, their bare feet slapping in rhythm on the cool wet sand. It was a bright hot day, the sun reflecting fiercely off the white sand and sparkling sea. Jim was silent, happy, still catching up on the awesome dimensions of the present, reveling in his good fortune, his mind already beginning to make bright plans for the future.

"I have to talk to you, Jim," Milly said. "Let's get off the beach."

In dappled shade under a palm tree, they lay in the grass and Milly told him as gently and as honestly as she could about the Frenchman. Jim, listening, admired her the more, appreciating her dilemma. He'd had five weeks at sea to come to know his mind. He was giving her one day. "And I have to make the most crucial decision of my life. Oh Jim, I need time to sort myself out. I want to go to a church."

She wanted to know if he really knew what he was doing, if he really wanted her. "You don't know me, Jim. You know what they say, a whore is always a whore."

He reached out his hand to rub her cheek, saying, "You're acting. Stop acting."

He felt a sublime arrogant confidence that she would choose him. He did not doubt that she loved him. And did she not know how much he loved her?

As they left the beach on their way to the bus stop, she said miserably, "Oh Jim, are you disappointed in me?"

"No, of course not. I respect your honesty."

"I'm sorry if I disappoint you. This is all happening so fast."

When they went into the church, Jim had smugly assumed that he had God on his side. They knelt together and prayed. Jim prayed in thanksgiving for everything that had happened that day and asked God's blessing on Milly and himself.

The church was crowded with worshippers. There was a priest fussing about in the sanctuary. A gold monstrance stood on the altar.

"They're going to have services," Milly whispered to him.

"No, it's just exposition of the Blessed Sacrament," he said and with cruel stupidity he added, "Were you ever an altar boy?" and he saw her stiffen, knew he had hurt her, hurt her badly, and searched for words to make amends and knew there were none, so he sat in miserable silence thinking, Oh God, forgive me.

"Let's leave," Milly said.

They walked away from the church, their hands joined, and then suddenly turned and embraced each other and kissed.

They crossed the street to an Indian restaurant and Milly ate another big meal while Jim, still with no appetite, smoked cigarettes and drank tea.

Back at Jackie's house, Jim excused himself ostensibly to take a shower but really to let the two sisters talk alone.

When he came back, they both began telling him how good the Frenchman was to them. Then Jessie came in with some dope and they went out on the balcony to smoke it.

And out on the balcony under the sky and palm trees Jim began the battle of his life. Milly marshalled before him all the reasons why they should not be lovers. She accused him of not thinking seriously about his decisions, demanded to know in practical terms how he planned to support them. He fought back as best he could, his life teetering in the balance, pleading his case, sometimes coming on strong and sometimes appearing weak and foolish. Ultimately he left it in her hands. It was she alone who knew her own feelings for him. She alone who would decide what she would do with her life. And him.

She softened finally, came to sit next to him, under his arm. "Don't be nervous, Jim. You're so tense."

"I am tense. I feel like I'm in combat."

"Jim, Jim, you've been so good to me. You gave me the happiest days of my life."

"Yeah, yeah," he said, waving his hand in weary dismissal. He did not want to hear about the past. He only wanted to learn what his future would be. He went back to pleading his case, asking her to give him the chance to know her, to give themselves the chance to work out their lives together.

"I would want more," she said. "I would want your name."

"My name? Marriage?"

She nodded. "Yes."

He exhaled a long breath. "Sure. Though after living with me a while, you may decide you don't want it."

Marriage was something final and irrevocable. He would not hesitate once they truly knew and accepted each other.

"Let's go inside," she said. "This conversation has become too serious."

Then they were out in the night time street, he feeling drained, weary. They ordered food to take home to Jackie who was recovering from her operation and ate big bowls of mutton soup. Jim wolfed it down with his old appetite. "I think I'm feeling better," he said. On their way back to Jackie's house Milly said, "I just want to go home and take a long shower and be alone to do some thinking."

They made plans to go to the beach the next day.

"I'll come by and meet you in the morning," she said. "What time do you want me to come?"

"Five."

She laughed. "Five in the afternoon?"

"Anytime, baby. Come as early as you can."

Back at the house, they woke Jackie up for dinner. Jackie returned to bed. Jim helped Milly clear the table. Then she was in the kitchen washing dishes as Jim sat thinking on the sofa.

As she waited for her cab to come, she said to him,

"Whatever happens, Jim, whatever I decide, I promise you a good time. We'll have a good time in Singapore like before."

But he did not want to hear anything about good times if she decided against him.

Then the taxi arrived. Outside the door, he held her in his arms and kissed her. And then she was gone.

There remained only the last act to be played out. The scene was the balcony of Jackie's house. Jim sat in a beach chair, playing his guitar. He wore only a pair of shorts, ready for the beach, waiting for Milly to come. It was a bright hot morning. He had fallen into a deep dreamless sleep the night before and felt rested now, calm, at ease with himself. He waited only for the chance to be alone with Milly out on the beach.

When a car pulled up the driveway, a bearded white man at the wheel and Milly in the passenger seat, Jim know the game was over and he had lost.

Strangely calm, he kept playing his guitar, waiting for the last scene to be played out, already knowing the result, knowing she had made her choice.

Her choice had been between being Jim's woman or staying a whore. For she did not love the Frenchman but was merely being kept by him, bedded in his air-conditioned home and driven about in his car and bedecked with the clothes and jewelry the Frenchman's money bought, who unlike Derek did not throw temper tantrums nor beat her nor even particularly speak much to her and most importantly and best of all he was often away and she was free to whore on Bugis Street.

It was this that galled and rankled him and filled him with baffled rage: that for a time she had been tempted to be free, to abandon her old life, to leave the Frenchman's dollhouse and to choose as an independent woman, out of the feelings of a woman's heart, to begin a new life with Jim, and that finally she had chosen to remain a whore.

For the last scene she played on the balcony showed no style or grace or class, with none of the customary tact a normal woman would show for the wounded feelings of her rejected lover. No, pathetically revealed as a cheap whore, she played that last scene badly.

After a suitable pause to build suspense, she appeared out on the balcony, came out on stage with her Frenchman in tow, injecting a useless third character into a drama meant only for two. Yes, the rejection of Jim's love was to be a public event. She had not the grace to allow him to make a quiet exit, the nuisance presence of the Frenchman thus limiting Jim's repertory of response, reducing the sad tragedy of love's betrayal to the silly dimensions of a drawing room farce, as she smugly introduced the two suitors to each other and then airily informed Jim, the spurned lover, that she was going shopping and then to lunch with the Frenchman.

It was the first time he had known her to act clumsily, stupidly, showing all the normal social graces of an ignorant whore. She had put him in a cruelly intolerable bitterly humiliating situation and then had the blind shameless stupidity to ask him to remain in it, to "hang around" as she put it.

No, he had no choice but to leave, and stay away, for suddenly she had become poison to him.

"You're staying with the Frenchman then," he said when they were alone.

"Yes."

"What made you decide this? When did you decide?"

"This morning. What can I say to you?"

"Nothing. There are no words."

"Jim, please. I'm only a woman. Please try to understand."

"Milly, you sure don't make it easy. What do you want me to do?"

"Hang around. If you want."

"No. I'm leaving. There's no sense in my staying in Singapore, is there?"

"Where will you go?"

"I don't know."

"Write to me."

"No, I just want to forget you."

"I guess I overestimated you," he said.

"Perhaps you underestimated me," she replied.

"Whatever," he said hopelessly, waving his hand in weary defeat.

Perhaps he did underestimate her. And overestimate himself. Perhaps he was not worthy of her love, no reason to demand she abandon security for his madness, frenzied dreams, crazy schemes. She simply did not believe in him, nor, God knows, love him, and nor in the end seeing his naked and pathetic need for her, did she have any respect for him, no, and precious little pity for his ridiculous hurt.

But perhaps she was not so complex. She was better dressed now, fatter, happy as she stays with her Frenchman and his car and his air-conditioning. Was she never really tempted to love Jim? To risk herself with the crazy gringo? Perhaps the Frenchman just outbid him. She may have simply seen that Jim was a dangerous financial risk.

Or could it be that Jim blew it, came across as too strong, too crazy, shocked and scared her, baffled and hurt her? He had been good to her in his time and place but was now a damned nuisance. She could not afford to jeopardize her position with the Frenchman, would be crazy not to play it safe now so close to her operation and with her sister still sick. And as for Jim's love, who needs it?

"Take care of yourself. You've made your decision. I just hope you don't come to regret it."

"I won't regret it. There is no such thing as regret. You just keep on living."

"Yeah. Well. Take care of yourself."

"I will. You too. Take care," she said, and turned, and walked away.

In the end, she had the sense, the grace, not to kiss him, nor to touch him.

Epilogue

Already slipping back now into the comfortable poses and masks of his old personality, ready now to retreat back into the old rambling savage life of speed and drinking and taking pleasures where they may be, Jim reflects ruefully that it should be some years till the cycle turns again, till he is so heartily sick of himself that he will gamble again, hurl himself outward toward a woman, relying on her mercy, demanding her understanding. His old self is already laughing at the romantic fool who fell in love with Milly Visweswaran.

Yet this is only partly true. He is not, cannot be, the same man he was before meeting Milly. A heart opened, blasted open in love, cannot be closed so tightly back again, or at least it would take years of bitter and solitary effort to try. And, strangely, he feels no real bitterness, nor can even complain of being lonely. His new resiliency, strength, calm acceptance of his lone freedom, strange lack of self pity, he can certainly trace to the example and influence of the Singapore girl. And as much as he would search for blame for the failure of their love, he knows the deeper he searches the more evidence he will dredge up against himself.

And he longs to say to her that he would like to stay her friend. To offer what help he can bring.

What hurt she inflicted on him really compares as nothing to the immense gift of herself that she gave him. He is grateful for having known her. He will always love her and, God knows, try to understand.

TEN
YEARS
LATER

Ten
Years Later

... I fell in love with Milly again. This time, from a distance. I was living in Songkhla, a fishing town on the Gulf of Thailand, six hundred miles north of Singapore. Not that I thought Milly was still living in Singapore. I figured she'd had the operation and was married and living in Europe, if not with the Frenchman then someone else. She had the drive and beauty and charm to be anyone or anywhere.

I had a Thai wife now and two daughters, eight and six.

In June 1976, my bride Mem and I had ridden a motorcycle from Songkhla down through Malaysia – Penang, Cameron Highlands, Malacca – to Singapore for our honeymoon. Mem was a country girl and had never seen a department store or ridden on an escalator. She loved Bugis Street. Jackie still favored silk catsuits and Tina gauzy evening gowns, but Sarah had gone cheekily downscale in cut-off denim short-shorts, bare midriff, blouse knotted under heavy breasts. I studiously ignored them and they returned the courtesy.

Mem and I settled in Mobile, Alabama, where I finished a novel about my civil rights days in Birmingham in the summers of 1965 and 1966. A year later, we moved back to Songkhla. I got an English teaching job at the local university. In June 1980, I started work at the American Consulate as de facto vice consul. My main job was to write cables reporting on the Vietnamese boat people who were washing up along the coast. A camp on the beach in Songkhla housed up to ten thousand refugees and they became the fodder for a new novel called *Boat People*.

In 1985, the Consulate got its first computer, a Wang with those early floppy disks. Using this I transcribed and printed out the sea journal I had kept while on the boat with Erik. This led me back to the smudged carbon copy of *Singapore Girl*, which I hadn't read in years.

And suddenly I was in love again. I was back with Milly in Singapore in 1975 and I could see her face and hear her laugh. Whitney Houston's "Didn't We Almost Have It All" had just come out and I would sit at the local expat bar wobbly with nostalgia for the second great love of my life and wondering whatever became of Milly.

I gave Milly the original copy of *Singapore Girl*. That was the whole purpose of writing it – to impress her and win her back. I wrote Part One over thirty-six hours in a windowless back room in the Sing Ho Hotel, an old Chinese mansion on Mountbatten Road in Katong. One rainy night I took a taxi to a bar in Changi frequented by the Argyll and Sutherland Highlanders to score dope. That accounts for the loosening of the narrative in Part Two. After three more days, I had a typed manuscript of eighty-seven pages, one-and-a-half spaced with no margins – twenty-five thousand words. Then I called Jackie's house to find Milly.

I was sitting on Jackie's bed when Milly came in and quickly sat in a chair by the door. We exchanged nervous greetings. She was dressed in her usual street clothes: blue jeans and a long-sleeved muslin shirt.

Tina poked her head around the door. She wore a faded yellow sarong hitched over her breasts.

"Hi, Jim! Welcome back!"

"Thank you."

"What are you doing later?" Milly asked her.

"I'm going to sell my pussy," Tina said sweetly and left.

There was an awkward silence.

I handed over my gifts: a travel Scrabble game, a dictionary. Then I gave her the manuscript.

"This is about us," I said. "If I were a painter, I'd give you a painting. If I were a musician, I'd write a song for you. I'm a writer, so this is all I can give. It's the only copy and it's for you."

She sat with her legs crossed high and her hands daintily folded over her knee. I saw now, with brutal clarity, that her hands were big, and her feet, and her shoulders.

She took the manuscript in silence, flipped it open, and smiled.

"Singapore Girl. That's me? Thank you." She lifted her hands and sang the jingle from the Singapore Airlines commercial which glorifies the mystique of their sarong-clad stewardesses: "Singapore girl, you've got a way about you …"

Her voice was unexpectedly deep.

"Do you have a cold?" I asked.

She looked bewildered. "No. Do you know one of our girls had the operation and became a stewardess for Singapore Airlines? Her name is Cynthia and she's a very tall, very beautiful Chinese girl …"

Milly's eyes lit up and her hands began dancing their magic as she launched into the story of Cynthia. Her fingers were long and slender, tipped by long pink nails, and whatever they did – rolling a joint, smoking a cigarette, peeling a mango, skewering a satay stick – they moved with an elegant, languid grace.

She snapped back in focus and she was beautiful again. I hardly described what she looked like in *Singapore Girl* – my title did indeed come from the airline commercial – because I was writing the story for her and she already knew what she looked like. Just like I didn't mention much about my past because I had already told Milly everything through placid hours of holding hands and talking. We held hands everywhere except when, in taxi cabs and coffee shop booths, I had my arm over her shoulders. And whenever we found a quiet spot – in Tiger Balm Gardens, the Singapore Museum – we'd sneak a tight clinch and a tongue-churning kiss

What did she look like? She was petite: five foot two, 120 pounds. My nickname for her was Boney Wog in retaliation for her calling me Fatty (Fat-*tay*) because I had a beer gut. She'd been taking birth control pills since she was sixteen, giving her a pert butt and cupcake sized breasts with thick black nipples. Again, she didn't need to be told that.

She had an unruly mop of thick black curly hair that tumbled down in two wings over her oval cheeks, over her shoulders and halfway down her back, held loosely at the nape of her neck by a bright silk scarf. From her Dravidian ancestors in India she inherited thick eyebrow ridges and, her only physical flaw, she'd plucked her brows into pencil-thin Greta Garbo lines, an unlikely feminine touch to the heavy bones of her forehead. But who noticed this when you looked into her big round eyes, those black limpid pools bright with intelligence and humor? Her eyes were perfectly framed by high cheekbones that tapered down to a small chin and plump delicate lips, instantly parted by the strong white teeth of her smile.

How much *fun* she was! Each morning, in her happy-go-lucky way, she lay out the options for another day's adventure in Singapore, always adding, "I'm easy."

The solemn Faulknerian rhetoric of *Singapore Girl* is misleading. I'd been rereading *Absolam, Absolam!* in Jakarta and I figured that stuff would wow her.

She wasn't particularly wowed.

"You should have told me these things before, not kept it in," she said the next day at the Sing Ho Hotel. The old mansion had a big front lawn and a gazebo where Milly, fearless as ever, lit up a joint.

"Jim, are you sure there's only one copy?"

"I swear. I wrote it only for you." (Hell, in those days, I made carbons of my letters).

"Because you wrote some very shocking things about Jackie."

"Well, I had to work through Jackie to get to you."

"I wouldn't want anyone else to read this."

Her respectable brothers were ashamed of Milly and Jackie. The sisters avoided the Queen of the Queens beauty contest or having their photos taken for Bugis Street postcards.

"You have my word," I assured her.

"And what about me becoming the Devil when I was getting ready for Bugis Street? That was spooky."

"Well, I was overwrought."

We crossed Mountbatten Road into a park and then on to the Ambassador Hotel, holding hands naturally, but when we settled down at the coffee shop for lunch, she sat at the opposite side of the table rather than under my arm. We were tense at first but soon warmed up with laughter. Milly surprised me by ordering a beer.

"I'm fattening myself for the slaughter," she explained. "My mother's resigned to the operation. She told me she had a dream where I appeared before her dressed as a boy but I told her that's never going to happen. So I'm all set now. I don't need to go to Bugis Street anymore. I'm so tired of tourists inviting me their tables and asking me the same questions. I give them a different answer each time. And the men are always so scared. They've never been with a girl like me before. Well, that's all over with."

A little giddy from the joint and the beer, we strolled hand-in-hand out to a narrow beach which was covered with trash and sea-wrack. We played an impromptu game of softball, me tossing coconut husks to her and she batting them out of the park with a stout log. Then we settled down in the sand under a palm tree and Milly delivered her verdict. She was staying with the Frenchman.

I pleaded my case, staring deep into her eyes, and she stared right back, resolute. She was studying French, she would travel to Paris, she would make her own life. I had to understand her.

I was better looking than either of my rivals and Milly certainly had a lot more fun with me. I cut a romantic figure with my sailboat and my guitar and my rousing tales of Africa and the Amazon. But the Frenchman had a car and a steady job on the offshore oilrigs. What did I have? I didn't even have a sailboat anymore.

"I could play my guitar for a living," I suggested.

Milly waved this notion away. "Jim, don't you know you're living in the most expensive city in Asia?"

Defeated, I lapsed into silence and looked out at sea. Erik was somewhere out in the Indian Ocean on his way to Africa and, like an idiot, I was stuck here. Where I wasn't wanted.

We stood up to go. I put my hands on Milly's shoulders and gazed down solemnly at her.

"One thing I forgot to mention in the story. It's very important."

"What?"

"I'm sorry I left it out now."

"What is it?"

I reached down and squeezed her plump denim-clad buttocks. "You've got a gorgeous ass."

"Oh, *you*!" she laughed, slapping my hand away.

The rest was anticlimax. I knew it was over but couldn't resist the need to see her again. The Frenchman was still on the rigs so we did indeed wind up "hanging out".

She took me to a fancy French café outside a five-star hotel on Orchard Road. For once she wore a dress: a short black number with red polka dots and spaghetti straps. I told her about the novel I had started writing. The idea had come to me on the boat in the Karimata Sea, heading south for Jakarta: what was I doing ten years ago? In the summer of 1965 I'd been a Catholic seminarian working in a voter registration campaign in Birmingham. Now I was trying to bring back long-vanished people and places.

Milly told about her own people and places that had vanished. Her old neighborhood of wooden houses had been obliterated and turned into public high rise apartments. The woods and streams where she and her Chinese and Malay friends had played were long gone too.

Milly seemed nervous, not quite looking at me, her eyes roving to the surrounding tables filled with rich tourists.

"That table next to us. I was sitting there a couple months ago, wearing this same dress, and I let myself get picked up, didn't I? An old German guy, a guest at the hotel, he picked me up and we went up to his room but he threw me out when he found out who I am."

I felt a piercing stab of sympathy for Milly. No matter how beautiful she looked and how much I adored her, she was always worried about her appearance: "How do I look?" She was always aware – balls stuffed up her body cavity and dick tucked backward into her crotch by a tight elastic G-string – that she was a fraud. I simply saw Milly, the beautiful object. She was the tightly constrained subject. The joy was mine, the pain hers.

Her mood suddenly brightened.

"But I've had my triumphs, Jim. Months before you came into my life, I had a steady customer, a rich Chinese named Kenny, who invited me to a big social ball. He gave me the money to buy a formal gown and shoes. He even lent me his mother's jewelry. I spent all day getting ready, my hair, my makeup. I was so nervous. Kenny picked me up and drove me to Raffles. A big ballroom filled with rich people! I was so scared as Kenny took me by the arm and introduced me to people. But you know what? They loved me! I was Eliza Doolittle!"

The next day Milly invited me for lunch at Jackie's house. It was Lisa's birthday and she'd invited a dozen queens to cut the cake. I was the only man. Afterward, I sat down at the dining table to join Milly and Jessica in a game of – what else? – Scrabble. Jessica was an old alumni of the house. A raven-haired, sloe-eyed Malay, she was totally feminine and self-possessed. She'd had the operation a year ago and was living with her American fiancee, an English teacher. She was back to Lisa's house for old time's sake but would eventually fly off to America and disappear into the real world, with no one ever knowing of her past. She'd finished her noviciate with the sisterhood where you lived as a woman and, in the end, became one.

Milly would soon be leaving the scene too. I was heartsick I could never touch her again, furiously jealous of the Frenchman who would one day make love to her as a woman.

Joining us at the game were two young queens whose names I forget. One had just had the operation and squirmed atop a foam cushion, a medical dildo up her new cavity. The pair were a type. Shrieking, squealing, giggling, scatter-brained, hands flapping and fluttering around their faces, they dithered endlessly over the game. Milly and Jessica sighed and rolled their eyes.

This would have been my world too, Milly's friends mine. In this strange reverse sorority, what all guys wanted at puberty – beard, biceps, broad shoulders – were anathema to them. Milly pitied Jackie for her height and bulk. "But I'm small!" she cried once, hugging herself delightedly.

A couple nights later we went back to our old hangout, the open-air Palm Beach, tearing apart chili crab and prawns, dunking chunks of bread into the hot sauce. Then a huge rain came crashing down and we ran out to the road and caught a taxi to Milly's new place. We played Scrabble and got very stoned. She showed me photographs the Frenchman had taken of her striking model's poses in a flower garden, dressed in a lilac evening gown.

"I went back to Bugis Street last night, didn't I?" Milly announced airily. "An Englishman named Neville picked me up and took me back to his house to meet his wife. We had a threesome on their waterbed. I played the boy with his wife. Then he told me to go but it was really his wife who wanted me to leave."

157

I was horror struck. She was impervious to how deeply she could shock me.

"Don't you know how much this hurts me?" I pleaded. "After the operation, why don't you go back to school and get a job? Why do you always have to sink to the lowest common denominator?"

She said nothing for a while, then calmly opened a tin of breath mints and offered me one. Subject closed.

It was only ten years later, while writing notes for a novel to be called *Bugis Street Blues* starring Milly and me, that the obvious occurred to me: Bugis Street was her home, her stage, the place where she was happiest. Every night she got to doll herself up before the mirror and don a slinky evening gown and sashay down the catwalk, meet up with her friends and gossip and regale each other with their conquests of the night before, all the while being ogled by all those men.

What a thrill it must have been for a seventeen-year-old repressed Catholic schoolboy to be suddenly released into the wild randy world of the queens – confronted with a new pick of virgins every night!

The night of my own deflowering was not quite as I described it to Milly – all that high-flown romance about the sailor home from the sea. Jackie turned a dozen or more tricks a week and getting a man into and out of her bed was down to a routine. The drill with me went like this:

Right after she told me her name, I asked, "Can I spend the night with you?"

"If you can pay my price."

"What's that?"

"Sixty Singapore."

There was the cuddling in the cab and the classic swaying of the rump before my eyes as we climbed the stairs to her bedroom. She turned on the light: queen sized bed, big mirror over a dressing table heaped with makeup and a wig stand. She turned her back and said, "Unzip me."

She disappeared down the corridor to a bathroom to lubricate herself and came back wearing a white baby doll negligee and holding a white towel between her legs. I was still sitting like an idiot on the bed.

"Take off your clothes," she ordered. "And get into bed."

I obeyed and slid naked under the covers. She slid in next to me and slowly untied the ribbons of her negligee to reveal her plump breasts. I sucked delightedly on black nipples as thick as a fingertip. "I want to suck your cock," she said and went down on me, stiffening me so hard, it was painful. Then she said, "Let's fuck."

We lay together talking afterward, me weak with gratitude, and suddenly I was hard again and pumping madly inside her, graced with the stamina of a porno star.

This is going to be a long and wonderful night, I

thought, but she was soon on her feet, saying she had to get back to Bugis Street to turn another trick. From the makeup table, she plucked a black elastic G-string and blue ruffled panties. She squatted down, tucking between her legs, and in one practiced motion, pulled G-string and panties up over her hips.

"It's very uncomfortable," she said. "You never get used to it."

Milly always wore her G-string, even when sleeping, or at least with me. She took it off only to replace it with a towel when we made love. One night when we were curled up together in the forepeak of the boat, I slyly reached into the G-string and, sure enough, encountered a smooth silky shaft. Milly yanked my hand away and slapped it.

On this my first night in this new strange world, Jackie left me alone with a big bottle of Anchor beer and copies of *Playboy* and *Playgirl*.

That's it, I thought. *I'm queer. I'm a fag.*

But I took some relief in that I really did prefer the *Playboy*.

There came the final farce with the "steady customer" – "Go ahead and fuck her. You can fuck her in the ass." – and I said goodbye to Jackie and headed down the stairs. The house had been dark when we arrived but was now ablaze with lights and music and people moving around. Facing each other across a coffee table, barechested in sarongs, two Englishmen sat chatting and drinking beer. Snuggled under their arms were two young queens, flowered sarongs hiked over their breasts. A scene as natural as could be.

This was a two-storied middleclass house in a suburban neighbourhood. The owner was Lisa, a rich pockmarked Chinese who made a rather unconvincing woman. Her room faced the front balcony, along with Jackie's. Tina, the tall Eurasian girl, had a room in the rear. There was another Chinese girl I saw only once in a cocktail dress, pearl necklace and stockings, talking on the communal telephone which stood on the staircase landing. "Of course, I love you," she was saying, staring at the tip of her cigarette. "I've always loved you."

During the day, queens were always drifting in and out of the house. Milly said they occasionally held "masquerade parties". One day, they were laughing about an orgy the night before in Lisa's room, bodies all over the bed and floor. They were friendly enough to me, joking about "Milly's new husband".

"This house gets so noisy," Milly said. "They get crazy when they're all together. I can only take so much of it. But they can be awfully funny."

This was her world and she had risen high in it. At the very pinnacle was Sarah, winner of the Queen of the Queens beauty contest, featured prominently on the postcards that vendors sold on Bugis Street.

Sarah shared a stucco bungalow with two other girls named Sheila and Nora. Nights, an old Chinese taxi driver would accept a cup of tea from Milly and talk about his grandchildren, then drive over with her to pick up the other girls for the ride to Bugis Street. The first night I rode with them, Sheila and Nora emerged from the house, elegant in evening gowns. Sheila slumped low in the passenger seat. I was in the back seat between Milly and Nora, the two of them bitching about how they always had to wait for Queen Sarah. At last, Sarah came sashaying down the walkway and jammed into the back seat with us. I was squeezed tightly amid silken thighs and sweet perfume. How do I get into these things? I asked myself, me the macho man from the Amazon.

Early in our romance, Milly and I had walked from Derek's house to Sarah's. It was nearly noon that first day when we reached Sarah's house. She was still sleepy-eyed, dressed in a short pink negligee. She sat before her dressing table, admiring herself in the mirror, bare shapely legs crossed, brushing her long red hair, talking with Milly in Malay and ignoring me.

"Isn't she beautiful?" Milly asked.

"Yes," I said, breathless.

"Would you like to make love to her?"

"No," I said quickly, bashful as a schoolboy.

If I'd said yes, would Milly have watched us? Or joined in? What did queens get up to when alone together?

Once Milly arranged for Sarah to join us at Changi Beach. We were lolling in the shallows – "Would you like me to play with you?" Milly asked, reaching into my shorts. "Oh, I'm such a randy bitch." – when we spied Sarah and her Australian boyfriend of the moment on the beach. Sarah wore a crimson bikini and quickly fell to brushing her hair. She and Milly got into a mock cat fight atop an overturned rowboat while I talked uncomfortably with the Australian, a young sailor named Bill, whom Sarah had lent money last time he was in port. He'd flown back now from Australia to pay her back. A few days later, Sarah dumped him, and then cried about it. Milly was worried about Sarah: she was twenty-seven, never had a steady boyfriend, still hadn't had the operation.

Sarah's great passion was traditional Malay dancing. Milly thought it would be a great idea if we invited Erik for a party to watch Sarah put on a show.

"I don't think so, Milly," I said as gently as I could. "She's not real."

And where was Erik in all this? Again, I left out a lot in *Singapore Girl* because Milly already knew all about Erik: growing up in the Panama Canal Zone, Peace Corps in Sierra Leone and again in the Philippines, sailing the boat with the owner from its Bangkok boatyard to Manila. The owner was a USAID honcho who arrived in Manila only to find out he's been transferred to Niger, West Africa. Which is why we were heading to Africa – to deliver the boat.

When I first rowed Milly out to the boat, Erik was

163

delighted, welcoming her with tea and cookies. I'd confessed about my walk on the wild side with Jackie but had no trouble passing Milly off as her sister. We passed around a joint and got giggly and off we went to Sentosa.

Erik liked Milly. She was as fearless as he was. Crossing over on the Sentosa Island cable car, they had insisted on lighting up a joint. All I could think was a cop on the other end and a Singapore jail cell.

Milly was asking us about Africa and the night life scene. "If I join you there, do you think Jackie and I could put on a lesbian show?"

Erik and I just looked at each other. Talk about the fast lane.

Erik was the daredevil of our Peace Corps group, always the first to jump off waterfalls and bridges, but I used to mock him for being bashful. Thanks to me and my guitar in a Manila bar, we'd wound up in a month-long romance with two rich teenage Cuban-American sisters. If I had not met Milly, I'd have mooched around Singapore doing what Erik did: eating cheeseburgers, watching movies, hanging around in hardware stores.

Most of the time, Erik was alone on the boat while I proudly squired Milly around Singapore. How much he resented this, I don't know. There were things we didn't talk about. Ultimately, though, he wasn't fooled by Milly. On the morning we left Singapore, Milly leaned up to kiss Erik goodbye, but he reared back with a knowing smile and put out his hand instead.

On the trip down to Jakarta, I kept a log in the form of a letter addressed to "Dear Boney Wog." I described to her what it was like to crash into a big log fish trap outside Singapore and lose our bowsprit, to surf along under bare poles in a shrieking horrific storm that blew us up toward Vietnam for five days, and how we lucked it back to Borneo where we found shelter up the river port of Pontianak where I wrote a thick letter and dispatched it to Milly. At the American Consulate in Jakarta, I found her own letter waiting, thanking me for the happiest time of her life, praying for my safety, hoping to meet again. That was all I needed.

Erik took my desertion well. It would mean a solo trip across the Indian Ocean, establishing his credentials as an ocean-going captain – "more glory" as he put it.

Erik soloed the *Quetzal* across the Indian Ocean, reaching the island of Mauritius in fifty-five days. "A record for slowness," he wrote later. On Mauritius he took on a Chinese shipmate who could not swim and 1,200 miles later was caught up in one of those legendary Cape of Good Hope storms and shipwrecked north of Durban. The *Quetzal* eventually washed ashore, but it was pretty well totaled. Erik got a job driving a bulldozer for a road construction crew in South Africa, then moved back to Manila to help build a ferrocement whaler for an American couple who planned to charter it to scuba divers in the

Marianas. They had promised Erik the captain's berth, but at the last moment anointed their son instead and gave Erik a plane ticket home. Feeling he had been used, Erik cashed the ticket and made his way south by tramp steamer through Mindanao and the Sulu Sea to Celebes where he came down with hepatitus. Six months later, celebrating his cure with his first beer, he wrote me a letter from Perth, Australia. He's found a job in a flour mill and was looking around for a new boat.

Within a year Erik was foreman of the mill. He bought a twenty-nine-foot racing sloop, rechristened *Isatu* after an old African girlfriend and planned to convert her into an ocean cruiser.

By now I was teaching at a university in Songkhla and one day a telegram arrived from Perth informing me that Erik Hansen had been killed in a motorcycle accident. By the cruelest of ironies, a letter from Erik arrived a few days later. His new boat was ready and he planned to leave Perth shortly. He had charts for the Gulf of Thailand, the winds and currents were favorable, and he asked whether I could find him a teaching job in Songkhla.

The friend who had sent the telegram followed with a letter of his own. Erik had a few beers in downtown Perth and was speeding home on his 750 BMW when he went off the road and hit a utility pole. He died instantly. The flour mill where he worked closed down for his funeral. Afterward, his former co-workers gathered at the local pub for an all-day booze-up and billiard tournament. "I don't know if you understand Australian character," the friend wrote. "But that was the highest tribute they could give."

Erik was fond of saying that we were very different: he was the practical one, I the dreamer. His ambition was to become a professional sailboat captain; mine to write a novel.

At sea, though, we did converge on one thing: God. There are no atheists in foxholes or small boats, especially in a big storm. Erik had returned to his Episcopalian faith after living for months with a Dutch Jesuit in a hill tribe village in the Philippines. On the boat we had Sunday services with the Book of Common Prayer. In thanksgiving for reaching Singapore safely, we attended Mass at St. Andrew's Cathedral.

Which brings me to another part of the endless puzzle of Milly, the Catholic part, the one most difficult to write about. She was only four years out of Catholic high school. I was only seven years out of a Catholic seminary where I'd spent years praying and meditating – lessons hugely reinforced by all those solitary nights under the stars at sea.

"We're both Catholics, both believe we're entering something sacred," I wrote ten years later. "Who is Milly at the end? She's on her own lookout, dreams of going to Europe and becoming a 'success'. But with me she could revert to innocence, to Catholic schooldays, could rove around town and show me the sights and teach me to eat. I gave her freedom, laughs, a ready ear and adoring eyes. I was offering love, but what could she do with that? When I came back from Jakarta, feverish and serious and disorientated and slavishly in love, did she let me go so as not to hurt me? She had just won her freedom from Derek and needed a financial arrangement – not another husband. Timing was off and I was off. Still, I believed how could she fail to love me, when so many others had? At our best, I loved her and she allowed herself to be loved. She showed me her best face and if she couldn't keep it up, neither could I. And if she broke my heart, it deserved to be broken."

There was ordinary time and there was sacred time: Milly time. I remember painting the stanchions on deck and singing at the top of my lungs "We may never love like this again!" – from the movie *Towering Inferno* which I'd seen with Milly the day before. My life was slow minute-by-minute drudgery until Milly's voice came: "Jim!"

Heart thundering, I literally leapt for joy. With that summons I was made whole and my life flowed with meaning again. There she stood on the seawall, smiling and waving. I jumped into the dinghy to pick her up.

We had the boat to ourselves. Milly brought food and helped me paint. We smoked dope, we made love, I played my guitar and sang her favorite song:

> "Like some Prince Charming I will bring you two
>   white steeds and dapple-diamond crowns
> And climb your tower Sleeping Beauty 'fore you even
>   know I left the ground
> Oh you can wear a Cinderella, Snow White, Alice
>   Wonderlanded gown
> Come watch the no colors fade blazing into pedal
>   sprays of violets of dawn."

On the table in the cabin, I showed Milly all my photos from New York, Sierra Leone, Brazil.

"Don't you know how lucky you are?" Milly cried. "To travel the world! That's what I'll do as soon as I've got my passport. How I envy you! You realize I've lived on this island all my life?"

There was a photo of me in a cassock and Roman collar, a pom-pomed biretta perched atop my head, taken by my parents on the day I entered the major seminary.

"Is that you?" Milly squealed in amazement.

"Sure is," I replied with an evil cackle. "C'mere, you want me to hear your confession?"

Milly collapsed in hysterics.

There was a photo of my first love, Celia Lebron, at her high school prom, me her date and the only white guy. Celia was a black Puerto Rican from a charismatic Catholic

169

family. I met her in the summer of 1968, the Summer of Love, when I was seminarian living in a Brooklyn slum. The hoodlum priest who was my mentor broke up our romance and I went back to the seminary. A year and a half later, the priest was shacked up with Celia.

I told Milly this story and the story of the smiling black woman in an Afro wig holding up a glass of wine in the courtyard of Rockefeller Center: Adama Wuri Bah, whom I'd picked up on the verandah of the City Hotel in Freetown, Sierra Leone, and lived with for six months in the Lower East Side before I left her for Brazil. She threw her hands up over her face and wept at the airport. And Edilzia Costa, the green-eyed mulata from Recife, grinning from the cab of a mud-splattered pickup truck on the Transamazonic Highway, the Queen of the Transa, chefe of the Instituto National de Colonisaseo e Agropecuaria, patron saint of landless peasants. I left her crying too.

That was the day Milly jumped to her feet and, with a scarf and my glasses and a ruler as props, sprang into an impromptu comedy shtick, impersonating teachers, policewomen, Indian movie stars, housewives, schoolgirls. I laughed, entranced, tears streaming down my cheeks till, breathless, I fixed her with an adoring stare and declared, "I'm falling in love with you."

She flicked her wrist in dismissal. "Don't be silly," she said.

The day after my "lowest common denominator" sermon, I went with Milly to visit Jackie in the hospital. The deal had always been that Milly would take care of Jackie after her operation, then Jackie would take care of Milly.

After her operation, Jackie was fitted with a mould that would shape her new vagina. She took it out too soon, fucked and ruptured her innards. When I came back from Jakarta she was using a colostomy bag. I slept in her bed that first night.

"I can't fuck," she told me. "But I can give you a blow job."

"Aw, no thanks."

Now she was back in the hospital again for another operation. There was a whole ward of recovering queens, surrounding by friends and family.

Out in the street again, Milly and I strolled arm in arm in the rain while I sang, "Oh baby, baby, it's a wild world, hard to get by just upon a smile, girl." The Frenchman was back and she was going to have lunch with him.

Milly flagged down a taxi. We kissed and hugged.

"Goodbye, Jim."

"I'll be at Changi Beach tomorrow. I'll call. You don't have to come."

She shook her head. "Goodbye."

As the taxi moved away, I took a few steps toward it. "I'll see you, kid!" I cried desperately. She didn't turn her head.

171

The next day, standing in the rain, I called her from Changi Beach. No, she wasn't coming. I gave her my phone number.

"You call *me*, okay?"

"Yes, Jim. Goodbye."

I never heard from her again.

If you're going to endure three weeks of utter solitude, you can't beat the big sunny high-ceilinged front room of the Sing Ho Hotel. I moved there from the subterranean cell around the time Milly dumped me. Eight double-shuttered windows were arrayed in a semicircle. There were two beds, two dressers, two clothes cupboards, two hat-stands, a sink, a chair and a table upon which I set up my typewriter and banged out the first chapter of my Alabama novel about a hero priest in the first heady days of the Birmingham civil rights movement. I read the most important book in my life, *The Phenomenon of Man* by Teilhard de Chardin, the Jesuit paleontologist and mystic, For meals I walked a half mile to a food centre for mee goreng or mutton soup. Every night I sat in a Chinese café, read novels and drank a couple big bottles of Anchor.

I had a short romance with a Malaysian hooker I'd met in a seaman's nightclub near Clifford Pier. Her name was Fatima and she had a day job as a welder at the Jurong Shipyard – with burn marks on her fingers to prove it. She told me about her hometown, Malacca, and I decided that's where I'd head next. After three weeks, I wrapped up my first chapter, wrote a farewell note to Milly, and headed up to Malacca where I stumbled upon the Seaview Hotel and a jolly crew of Chinese, Malays and Indians who gathered nightly upon the rattan chairs of the ancient verandah to drink beer and stout and swap jokes with the barmaids. We were the Members, lah. I was among friends again.

I bought a motorcycle, a 250cc Honda XL Scrambler, and from time to time would ride it up to Kuala Lumpur or down to Singapore. Once, a few miles south of the Singapore causeway, I got caught in a ferocious monsoon downpour and passing the street where Milly lived, I pulled up at her house: 14 Palm Court. Soaked to the skin, I had a perfect excuse to see her, didn't I? I rang the bell. No one answered. And that was that.

Ten years later, in love with Milly again, I would write a fictional epilogue to *Bugis Street Blues*. I attach it at the end of this book. Once again, I failed to do her justice.

The second time I fell in love with Milly lasted maybe a month. I thought about her all the time, memories came flooding back, I wondered desperately what had happened to her. Where was she? What was she doing now? I even asked a friend who was heading to Singapore to look her up in the phone book. No Milly Visweswaran. Either she was living somewhere else or was listed under a married name.

The infatuation only broke when my wife and I joined a Thai-expat group of marine biologists on a two-week scuba diving trip to Koh Adang in the Andaman Sea. Returning back to the mainland, I saw a shipwrecked fishing trawler that gave me the idea for my third novel, a thriller called *Running with the Sharks*. I stuffed my notes for *Bugis Streets Blues* into the same envelope with *Singapore Girl* and never looked at them again.

THIRTY
YEARS
LATER

Thirty
Years Later

... I was an editor at *The Nation*, Bangkok's feisty English-language newspaper. For four years I'd been editing and laying out the editorial and opinion pages but now I was on the infinitely easier features beat.

I'd just delivered my seventh book to my publisher. My first, *Waylaid by the Bimbos*, came out in 1991. This was a collection of first person humor stories I'd written for the *Bangkok Post*: stories about my sea trip with Erik, revels in Malacca, down and out days in Songkhla. Milly rated barely a half page. I wrote about "stumbling into a rather improbable romance with a Tamil girl" and a comical account about the confrontation with Derek, ending with: "He got the last line but after he shipped out, I got the girl."

I probably wrote a hundred stories about my golden years in Songhkla which boomed during the '80s with an influx of expat oil workers on the offshore rigs. There was the ritual running of the Hash on weekends, volleyball on the beach, windsurfing, spearfishing and lots of parties. One thing I can say for sure: I gave my kids a happy childhood. There were four of them now.

In 1992, I moved up to Bangkok. The Consulate in Songkhla was closing down and I landed a job as Associate Editor of a great business-lifestyle magazine called *Manager*. The sequel of *Waylaid by the Bimbos* came out a year later: *On the Bus with Yobs, Frogs, Sods and the Lovely Lena* with forays to Cambodia, Laos, and Vietnam.

During five years at *Manager*, I wrote profiles of the whole gamut of Bangkok society: tycoons, slum dwellers, politicians, bargirls, boxers, truck drivers, ambulance attendants, models, architects, construction workers ... I got a book out of this called *Bangkok People* which reached #1 on the bestseller list.

Manager went belly up in the Great Bust of 1997. For a year I scrambled to keep my family fed. I wound up as a reporter on the *Phnom Penh Post*, covering the election and the street riots of July, 1998. I got a book out of this too: *The Year of Living Stupidly: Boom, Bust and Cambodia*.

By 2005, though, life was tranquil. I wrote a weekly book review and the occasional travel or humor story. I was a grandfather. My two younger kids were getting ready to go to college. I went sailing for a week every year at the Phuket King's Cup Regatta. On a Monday morning,

I was just settling down with my notes for my annual sailboat story when I flicked on my email.

"Singapore Girl" read the subject line. I opened it:

Please, see attached.
If you are the author, as I believe you are, I wish
to return to you this manuscript you wrote back in
1975 for Milly.

Attached was a scanned copy of a typewritten page:

"There is no sense in hating someone for not loving you …"

I sucked in a breath and stared bug-eyed at the screen.

There was a photo attachment too: a full color close-up of Milly staring right at me, smiling, eyebrows arched, dark eyes vastly amused, wild black hair tumbling down her cheeks.

I couldn't breathe. My face flushed and hands flew over my pounding heart. I hadn't seen her face in thirty years.

Under the photo were the words: "Singapore, 1975".

I scrolled down and another photo appeared: a fifty-year-old Milly, unsmiling, head bent, glancing up at the camera, face fuller, hair shorter, swathed in black.

The words: "Paris, April 7, 2004".

I stared at Milly for an eternity, in love again.

Finally, I forced my trembling fingers to draft a reply.

It was the Frenchman. His name was Alain Dumont and he had married Milly in May 1976. In August 1977, his oil company transferred him to work in the North Sea and he moved with Milly to a small studio apartment in Paris, near his parents.

"I had no doubt that it was you since, sometime last year, Milly asked me to try and trace you through the net," he wrote back to me.

"It was quite easy, and as soon as she saw your picture, she exclaimed, 'Yes! That's Jim!' and went on laughing wildly at your rather ample belly, bald head and thick beard.

"We sent an email to *The Nation*, with a couple of pictures, but got no feedback. I concluded that you probably never received it. She concluded that you were probably not interested. This time around, I found the transcript of an interview you gave (recently?) to M. Scott Murray, "The Odyssey of Jim Eckardt", in which you indicated your personal email address. I took the opportunity to look up the books you have written and I am considering reading one or two of them ...

"To tell you what happened to her since '75 would probably be a good subject for a very thick novel. In fact, it was one of her (sometimes hare-brained) ideas: write a book, or rather have it written, about her rich lifestory; and/or to have *Singapore Girl* published."

This was the start of a correspondence that lasted for

months. What I'm going to do here is put everything into a strict chronology.

Alain had first been Sarah's boyfriend and had leased her suburban house. Sarah, though, often flew into violent rages and Alain fled to another house which he later offered to Milly when she had to abandon Derek's place. There was supposed to be no sex but, of course ...

For her first two years in Paris, Milly had a hard time adapting. She had no friends. "But, on the other hand, while roaming around Paris alone (when I was working in the North Sea), her magnetism allowed her to meet and befriend all kinds of people who were fascinated by her at first sight, so all in all, she was quite happy."

Alain paid tribute to Milly's extraordinary strong will and pride and her Asian devotion to her husband. In time, she managed to feel comfortable in France.

Then Milly decided to make her own money. Jackie and Sarah were in Germany, making big money on the stripper circuit. Milly went to Switzerland and got a job as a hostess and stripper in a Geneva nightclub. Here she fell in love with a rich Swiss named Dominique and moved in with him.

"But that changed nothing about her feelings for me (and certainly not my feelings for her) and she would always call me whenever she had some problem or was feeling sad. In fact, at her request, I went approximately once a month to Geneva, staying at her boyfriend's place, and we formed a quite happy and friendly threesome (within acceptable limits, of course).

"Unfortunately, things started to turn terribly sour when her boyfriend's sister, and one of his friends, went to tell his parents (extremely rich and conventional Swiss family) 'who' she was, and that the bearded Frenchman who came regularly to visit was in fact her husband ... They literally kicked her out.

"She begged me to take her back, but this was not necessary since I could in no way foresee a life without her.

"Then at the end of '86, my company sent me back to work in Indonesia. At first, she decided to stay in Switzerland and carry on working, but three months later, she rushed back to be with me, and we lived in Balikpapan for the next eight years. During that time, we managed to buy a very nice little house in Singapore, one of her dreams."

They had a big house and a maid in Balikpapan and a lifestyle like my own in Songkhla with many of the same people, affectionately known as "oil field trash". I'm sure I had friends in Songkhla who knew Alain and Milly. If only I'd known to ask. Alain mentioned lots of parties, many of which she threw herself: "She loved inviting people over and spent a lot of time organising everything single-handedly."

In one email, Alain attached a portrait of Milly

by a famous Swiss painter, Jerome Gromfay. Entitled "Rani", Milly gazed impassively from an oval, long-nosed Mogdaliani face. Long black hair tumbled down her long neck, parting at the cleavage of her black dress. A blue bird with outspread wings nested on her head. Perched on her finger was a tiny top-hatted man with angel wings.

"She spoke about you once in a while, wondering what had happened to you," Alain wrote. "Especially when we were playing Scrabble, which we must have done a million times, on the Travel Scrabble game you had given her together with the Little Oxford, our only reference whenever we were playing the game, although we had other dictionaries. 'You know, Jim gave them to me ...' She always won, the very few times I did, I sometimes regretted it: she was a very bad loser: 'Can I make this word?' 'Sorry, it doesn't exist.' 'WHY NOT?'

"No, she never forget you. From the first, she told me she loved you, but you could not give her security. She was often talking about 'the three loves in my life': you, me, and her Swiss boyfriend Dominique.

"She didn't find it odd or incompatible to love several men equally. But the impact she made, the marks (scars?) she left on the men who were fortunate (unfortunate?) enough to cross her path are tremendous.

"It is clear from your messages that your feelings for her are still quite strong ...

"As for Dominique, sometimes after she left

185

Switzerland, he dumped everything, family, business and all, and went to live in Thailand for several years, building sailboats (he is a highly skilled carpenter). Then in 2002 or 2003, Milly went to Geneva again to try and find work, and she met him for old times' sake. Although nothing happened, sometime after that, we heard that he and his wife had broken up and he was preparing to come back to Asia again. He may be somewhere around right now, either in Thailand or Indonesia.

"Then there was this French TV producer who was madly in love with her and, among other things, had invited her to the 20th anniversary party of a leading French TV magazine at the Versailles Palace: 'Can you believe it, Alain, me, the insignificant little whore from Singapore, at the Orangerie, the ONLY colored girl in the midst of all these beautiful people, and all these men looked at me, fascinated?'"

Singapore Girl arrived by post, bound in a green-trimmed clear plastic binder, by Milly I guess. There was also a packet containing twenty-two photographs. Seven were small square 3 x 3 inch snapshots of Milly that I had completely forgotten taking, using Erik's little Kodak.

Milly posed on the boat's bowsprit, hands gripping a stay, thrusting out her plump little rump. Erik's captain's cap was perched on her head, bright blue scarf trailing below. She wore white chinos and a pink-and-white tie-dyed top, her bare mahogany shoulders agleam in the sun.

In a close-up, seated in the cockpit, she regarded me with a close-lipped smile. I could hear her voice again. What did she say just before I took the picture? What did she say afterward? No way of knowing now.

Then she was seated primly on a girl's bicycle: another day in Sentosa, wearing jeans and a white muslin shirt. In one, she was riding behind me, in a second, looking back behind, grinning. Then a final close-up, in profile, she is looking away, blue scarf wrapped around her head, tiny gold earrings, a fat joint held in fingers tapered with bright pink nails.

Then Alain's pictures, larger (4 x 7 inches) and better quality: the series of five of Milly posing as a model in a Singapore flower garden. A familiar black-and-white photo shows Milly at nineteen, staring to one side, wearing hoop earrings and same tie-dyed top she would wear on my boat two years later, her shoulders and upper chest bare. This was the only photo I had of Milly till my wife tore it up in Singapore on our honeymoon.

Then one marked "Switzerland c. 1980s": a studio portrait of Milly in her stripper costume – standing sideways in yellow high heels, her thin legs in white fishnet stockings, her hair shortened and permed like a flapper. White lace gloves nearly reached to her shoulders. She wore a white flimsy-fringed jungle dress and clutched a pair of blue-and-white feathered fans. She regarded the camera with a blank, purse-lipped pose.

Then it was 1984 and she was thirty years old and more beautiful than ever. In a solemn black-and-white portrait, she stares straight into my eyes. She'd let her eyebrows grow out and they frame those two perfectly-formed black pools of mystery.

Then it's ten years later, she's forty, and still beautiful, in three quarters profile, gazing sideways and up, red lipstick and matching nail polish, her fingers about to put a cigarette to her lips.

Then she's a plump handsome matron in Balikpapan, gold earrings and necklace, dressed in a blue silk Indonesian costume, standing between two Japanese flower scrolls. And now she's forty-six in France, caught in mid-laugh, looking down through amber-tinted glasses, her face fattened with age. Then she's in Sakrata, Libya, posing on the steps of the ruins of a Roman amphitheater, blue sky and the Mediterranean beyond. She's wide-hipped in orange harem pants, both hands waving a yellow scarf over her head.

A final shot shows Milly in a snowstorm, just about to break into a smile. She wears a brown overcoat, gloves and a man's ear-flapped cap. Alain's caption reads: "France, Feb 2004. Frozen!!" Unmistakably, clasped in her leather-gloved fingers, is a thick smoking joint.

Over the next weeks, Alain emailed me other photos he

had scanned. One took my breath away: Milly at Changi Beach in a sopping wet black shirt and tight black short-shorts, hair hanging in drenched ringlets, brown skin agleam in sunlight, shooting a mad grin at the camera. Milly at her best, exactly as I remembered her.

There was Milly drinking coffee on Bugis Street, heavily made up, in her favorite red silk evening gown. Milly posing against a palm tree in Alain's favorite dress, a short polka-dotted number exposing her slim brown thighs – the same she'd worn at the French café.

Then she was on her honeymoon in the French Riviera and Swiss Alps, dressed in a jeans and a striped jersey, her hair in pigtails, looking like a schoolgirl next to the burly bearded Alain.

"In the beginning she was like a little kid, always asking me questions: who, what, why, where?"

Milly at the Louvre, the Champs Elysees, Toulouse, Tours, Avignon, the castle walls of Carcassonne, and the cathedrals of Reims and Chartres. Milly at dinners with Alain's family, the only brown face amid all the white. Alain with Milly's family, the only white amid the brown. Milly in a gorgeous sari, hosting Alain's fortieth birthday party in Balikpapan, the guests the usual mixed salad of oil field trash nationalities. Milly at a costume party, dressed as a tiger in a skin-tight striped body suit, dancing with an African girl.

In 1991, they took a trip to India to visit one of her

sisters in Madras, another in Tamil Nedu. And now there's Milly in Indian dress in front of the Taj Mahal and the strand at Bombay and a cathedral in Goa. Milly at a Hindu temple in Bali, at Borobodur in Java, at Lake Toba in Sumatra. Milly on a beach in the Maldives, stunning in a brown-and-gold bikini. Her hips and breasts had filled out in her late twenties. Milly and Alain, with his father and her nephew, on a camping trip up the east coast of Malaysia. Milly snorkeling on the islands of Tioman and Langkawi, Milly in Malacca and Penang and Kuala Lumpur. Milly at Lourdes filling a bottle with holy water to bring back to her family in Singapore.

All the while grinning into the camera. And I grinned back at her, happy to see her so happy. She'd achieved her dream. She'd escaped Singapore. She'd travelled around the world for thirty years as a glamorous woman. She'd become a success.

All was not roses, of course. Milly was prone to bouts of depression and drunken rages. Alain would sit absolutely still as she tore around the house, snatching up things and smashing them to the floor. "But never her best things. She was drunk but not crazy."

Along with the twenty-two photos that Alain sent me was my last message to Milly, typed very faintly on a single sheet of notepaper:

September 10

Dear Milly,

How are you, baby? I'm on my way to Malacca tomorrow. I thought to telephone you but it would have been no good. I knew when I called you that last Sunday from Changi Beach, even as I gave you my telephone number, that I would not hear from you again and it is just as well I suppose. I do wish I hadn't been so intimidated by my own feelings for you, that I could have been more relaxed and cheerful around you. You were right, Milly, we would have been no good together. There would have been titanic battles of ego with me on the losing end because loving you, I was vulnerable.

I owe you a debt, baby. The outsurging of feeling that you inspired enabled me to write so many pages about you in that first week, and the impetus has not left me. My solitude has provided me the very conditions with which to immerse myself in my past, to live intensely with my ghosts, the people I knew, and have some compassionate understanding of exactly who they were and what happened to them. I have a fixed plan for the first half of the book, divided into ten chapters and telling the story of the sixties in America. I have twenty finished pages about Alabama and the early civil rights movement, the mass demonstrations in Birmingham, the bombing of the Baptist church and the deaths of four little black girls, you know, stuff like that. That's all Chapter One which I have finished and will start Chapter Two in Malacca.

I speak some Malay now, been studying two books and have gotten a lot of help from Fatima, the Malay girl who replaced you in my affections. But mostly my life has been a solitary one, lived day by day in this enormous room (I moved from the old one a month ago) on the second floor, this circular turret that dominates the Sing Ho Hotel has been mine this past month, the seven shuttered windows and view of the lawn and gazebo and Mountbatten Road and my life has pretty much fallen into a pattern of work in the morning, lunch down at the market, relaxing with coffee and a book afterward and to walk the half mile back to my room and continue writing till dark, then dinner and a beer at the café and reading in philosophy or studying Malay or writing some more. By keeping busy, working, my mind always active, I have come to enjoy my solitude and put it to good use. I hope to keep it up in Malacca.

But what of you, Milly? What news? When is the fattened calf being led to the slaughter? I am not going to preach to you again about your future.

Though I am as worried and fearful as ever about it. You are in so many ways an immature girl, a sort of teenage flirt, and your dreams are girlish ones that are bound to be shattered against the cold reality of Europe. Be that as it may, I know I have no right to preach.

I seem to recall a promise from you about writing. And I will hold you to it. Be my friend, write to me: Poste Restante, Malacca, and I will tell you of my adventures in Malaysia.

Jim

And now let Alain finish his story.

Jackie committed suicide in January 1995, overdosing on sleeping pills and booze.

"We were on holidays in France at the time, and Milly's very first words when she heard the news were: 'HOW COULD SHE DO THIS TO ME?'"

"Milly: generous to the extreme, unselfish, kind, gentle, open hearted, loving, dedicated …

"But also unbelievably self-centered (human, animals, plants, objects even HAD TO bend to her will), devious at times, certainly not a liar (she hated lies passionately) but extremely clever at ever so slightly distorting facts and words, to turn them to her own advantage, whenever she felt threatened, even in the most improbable ways.

"In the end, it feels so good to talk about her to somebody who was (and still is) so passionate about her."

Jackie was married for ten years to a German bodybuilder, tall, blond, blue-eyed, a decade younger than she. After they divorced, she kept looking for an identical substitute but never found one. "She was too demanding and guys quickly became scared of her. She could be very violent, and how can a guy feel when, systematically everyday, coming back from work, he is greeted by a 'So, who did you fuck today?'

Sarah also married a German and has been living in Berlin for twenty years. Lisa lived in the States for many years, married to an American, but returned to Singapore a few years ago.

Milly met Tina, the tall red-haired Eurasian girl, on a Singapore street in the late 1990s. Tina was in a very bad state with drugs and booze and begged Milly to take her away with her.

"By the way, also in the late '90s, Milly was walking down Orchard Road one afternoon with a friend (I was on a rig in Thailand) and coming out of nowhere appeared ... Derek, going down on his knees, crying, and begging Milly to forgive him and take him back! Of course she told him to get lost.

"In Jackie's house, there was also 'crazy Jessie', Chinese, skinny as a scarecrow, and totally bonkers, at least that's the image she projected. Don't know what happened to her.

"And a number of others, who come back to my mind as I write, some of whom may have come back to Singapore. I may be able to contact one of them from 'the old days', with whom Milly had become quite friendly lately (once in a while, they would go out together at night, 'to catch men.'

"Milly was so naturally feminine that nobody on earth would possibly ever suggest that she was not a biological female. Unlike most of the other Sisters, whose ways of talking, moving and general behavior, would give them away almost instantly, as if, although they wanted to be women and went though a lot to achieve this goal, they somehow wanted to make sure that ordinary people would recognize them for what they were; probably the 'provocative' aspect of Sisters' character."

In 1995, Alain began to have his own problems. His lucrative contract came to an end and he had to go back to working on the offshore platforms, mostly in Songkhla. His highflying days were over and he had to sell the house in Singapore and pick up a condo instead. Two years after the 1997 Crash, he was in real trouble. He was laid off and had to sell the condo and move back with Milly to France, They lived in "a small sad little house which I owned in a small and sad little village in France". He fell ill with depression that lasted three years.

A few months into our correspondence, Alain was cleaning up his computer when he found the email message that Milly had sent to my newspaper, written two years earlier in April 2003:

> *Dear Sirs,*
>
> *Could you please kindly forward the following message to M. JAMES ECKARDT who, I understand, is one of your columnists. If I am mistaken, please kindly let me know.*
> *Many thanks for your help.*

> *DEAR JIM,*
>
> *They say "curiosity kills the cat"; I wonder !!!*
> *I see that life has been very good to you, "with your big beer belly" !*
> *Send my blessings to your family.*
> *You must be wondering "what the hell, who is this ???"*
> *Remember Milly, the "Singapore Girl" ?*
> *You did not leave your manuscript with a blond Bimbo, you know ! You left it with me. It was the story about Jacqueline and me.*
> *I have lived in the South West of France for the*

past 3 years and I sincerely hope to hear from you,
that is, if you want to.

Your friend.
Milly

Soon afterward, Alain landed a job in Libya with a competitor of his former company. But after three months, he quit after his boss told him that Milly could no longer stay in Libya with him. They went back to the small sad village in France, with savings nearly shot, living on welfare.

"She started being more and more sad and depressed, although it was always difficult to tell how she felt, what with her frequent and wild mood swings. Turning fifty hit her hard.

"Finally, in September last year, I decided to sell that house and whatever we could, pack the rest, dog and all, and go back to Singapore to try and start anew. She was wild with excitement. We arrived here on April 9, found a very nice house to rent, arranged very neatly (that and cooking were her two main passions), and I started looking for a job, either in the oilfields or as a freelance technical translator.

"Then one night in June, after a heated (drunken) argument with one of her brothers (nothing unusual), we went back home and she started picking an argument with me (not unusual either), decided to go out again and told me just before leaving the house: 'I've lost. You can have everything. You'll never see me again. I'm a failure.'

"Since it was not the first time, and I knew from experience that she would always come back, I did not pay undue attention.

"Two days later, the police informed me that she had been found at 4 a.m. at the foot of an HDB block (where her brother lives); she had jumped from the eleventh floor.

"I have to stop here for now; there's so much more to say but I just can't right now."

Epilogue /2

Milly and I meet at an outdoor café in Singapore (or Paris?). She brings up the old manuscript.

"You still have it? I'm flattered."

"I've carried it all around, like a snapshot of my youth."

"Do you show it to people?"

"One or two. You can have it back, if you like. For a price."

"No thanks, Milly. It's yours for keeps."

"It would make a good story, though, wouldn't it?"

"Yes," I smiled. "It would, wouldn't it."